The Flickskinny Book!

by Jeremy

The Flickskinny Book!

20th Anniversary Special Edition!

The Flickskinny
20th Anniversary Special Edition
Copyright 2018
by Jeremy Long

All rights reserved. No part of this book may be reproduced or used in any manner without written permission of the copyright owner except for the use of quotations in a book review.

For advertising, licensing, orders, or other inquiries, please visit www.garbagefactory.com

The Garbage Factory
Athens, Georgia, USA

If you are unable to order this book from your local bookseller, you may order directly from the publisher or the author. Visit www.garbagefactory.com or www.flickskinny.com for information.

ISBN 978-0-9975227-6-1
10 9 8 7 6 5 4 3 2 1

WHAT IS A FLICKSKINNY?

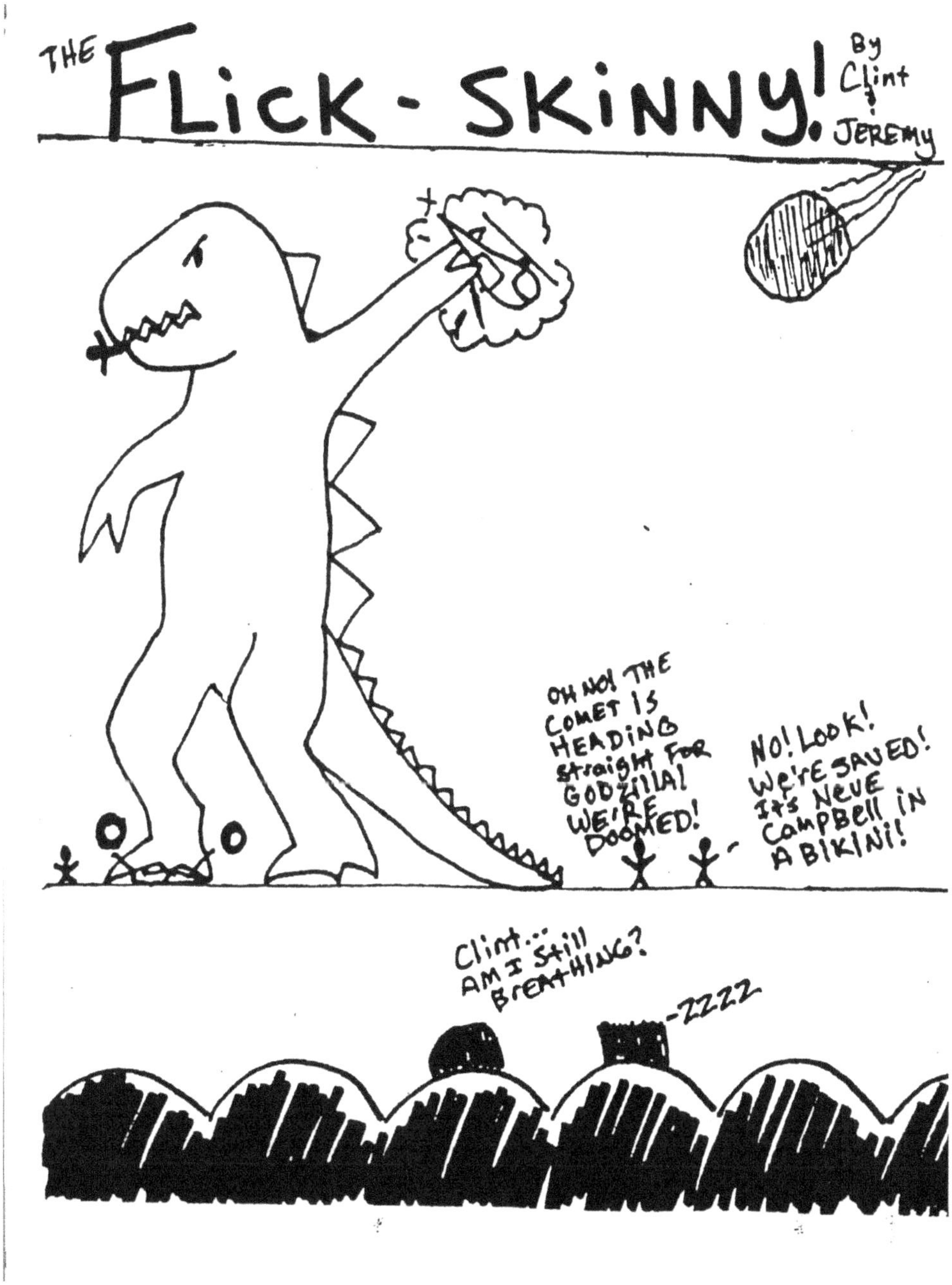
THE FLICK - SKINNY!
By Clint & JEREMY
OH NO! THE COMET IS HEADING straight FOR GODZILLA! WE'RE DOOMED!
NO! LOOK! We're SAVED! It's Neve Campbell in A BIKINI!
Clint... AM I Still BREATHING?
-ZZZZ

COMIC BOOK COVER-ISSUE #1-1998

THE HISTORY OF THE FLICKSKINNY

by Jeremy

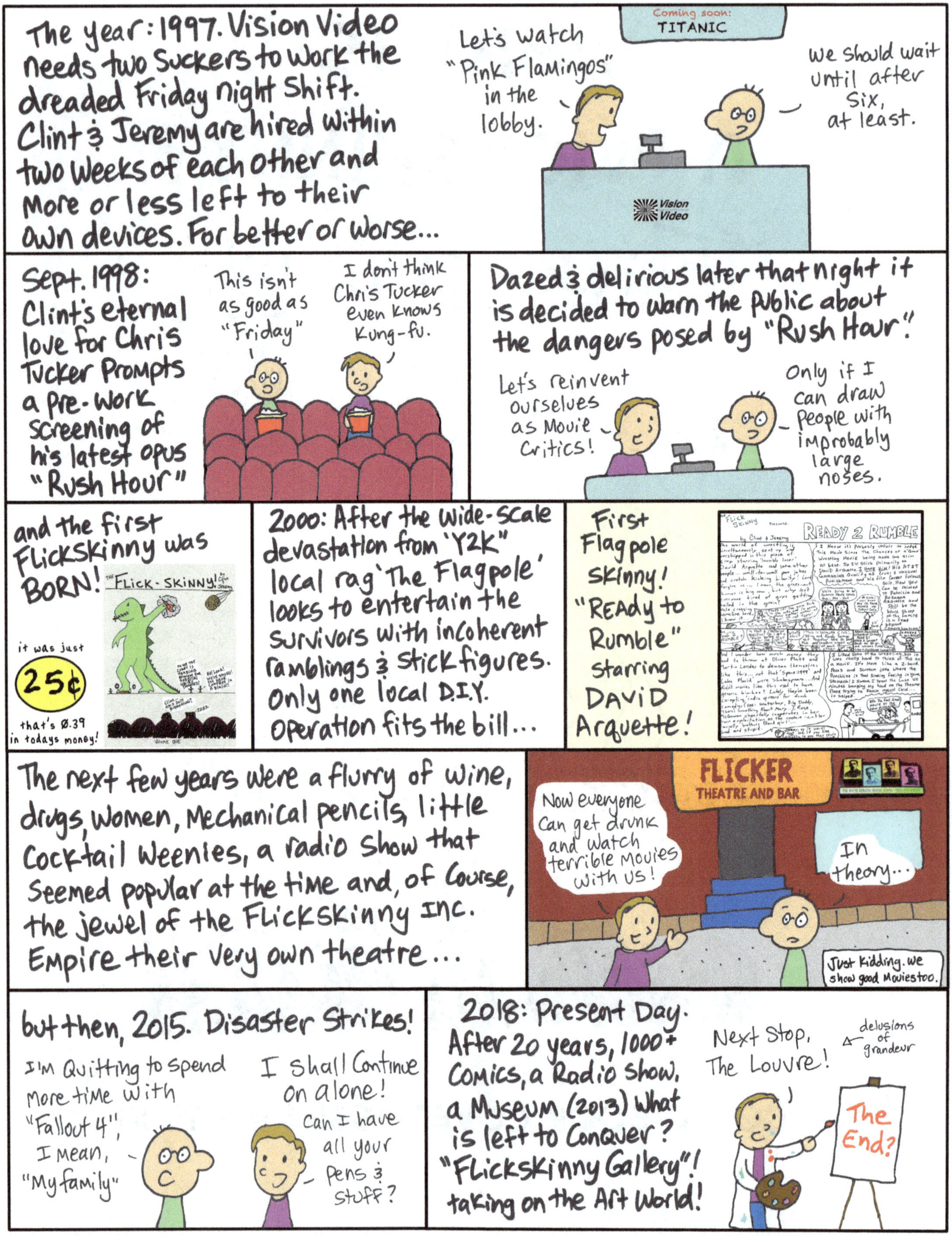
The year: 1997. Vision Video needs two suckers to work the dreaded Friday night shift. Clint & Jeremy are hired within two weeks of each other and more or less left to their own devices. For better or worse...
Coming soon: TITANIC
Let's watch "Pink Flamingos" in the lobby.
We should wait until after six, at least.
Vision Video
Sept. 1998: Clint's eternal love for Chris Tucker prompts a pre-work screening of his latest opus "Rush Hour"
This isn't as good as "Friday"
I don't think Chris Tucker even knows kung-fu.
Dazed & delirious later that night it is decided to warn the public about the dangers posed by "Rush Hour."
Let's reinvent ourselves as movie critics!
Only if I can draw people with improbably large noses.
and the first FlickSkinny was BORN!
FLICK-SKINNY!
it was just 25¢
that's $0.39 in todays money!
2000: After the wide-scale devastation from 'Y2K' local rag 'The Flagpole' looks to entertain the survivors with incoherent ramblings & stick figures. Only one local D.I.Y. operation fits the bill...
First Flagpole Skinny! "Ready to Rumble" starring David Arquette!
READY 2 RUMBLE
The next few years were a flurry of wine, drugs, women, mechanical pencils, little cocktail weenies, a radio show that seemed popular at the time and, of course, the jewel of the FlickSkinny Inc. Empire their very own theatre...
FLICKER THEATRE AND BAR
Now everyone can get drunk and watch terrible movies with us!
In theory...
Just kidding. We show good movies too.
but then, 2015. Disaster strikes!
I'm quitting to spend more time with "Fallout 4", I mean, "My family"
I shall continue on alone!
Can I have all your pens & stuff?
2018: Present Day. After 20 years, 1000+ comics, a radio show, a museum (2013) what is left to conquer? "FlickSkinny Gallery"! taking on the art world!
Next stop, The Louvre!
delusions of grandeur
The End?

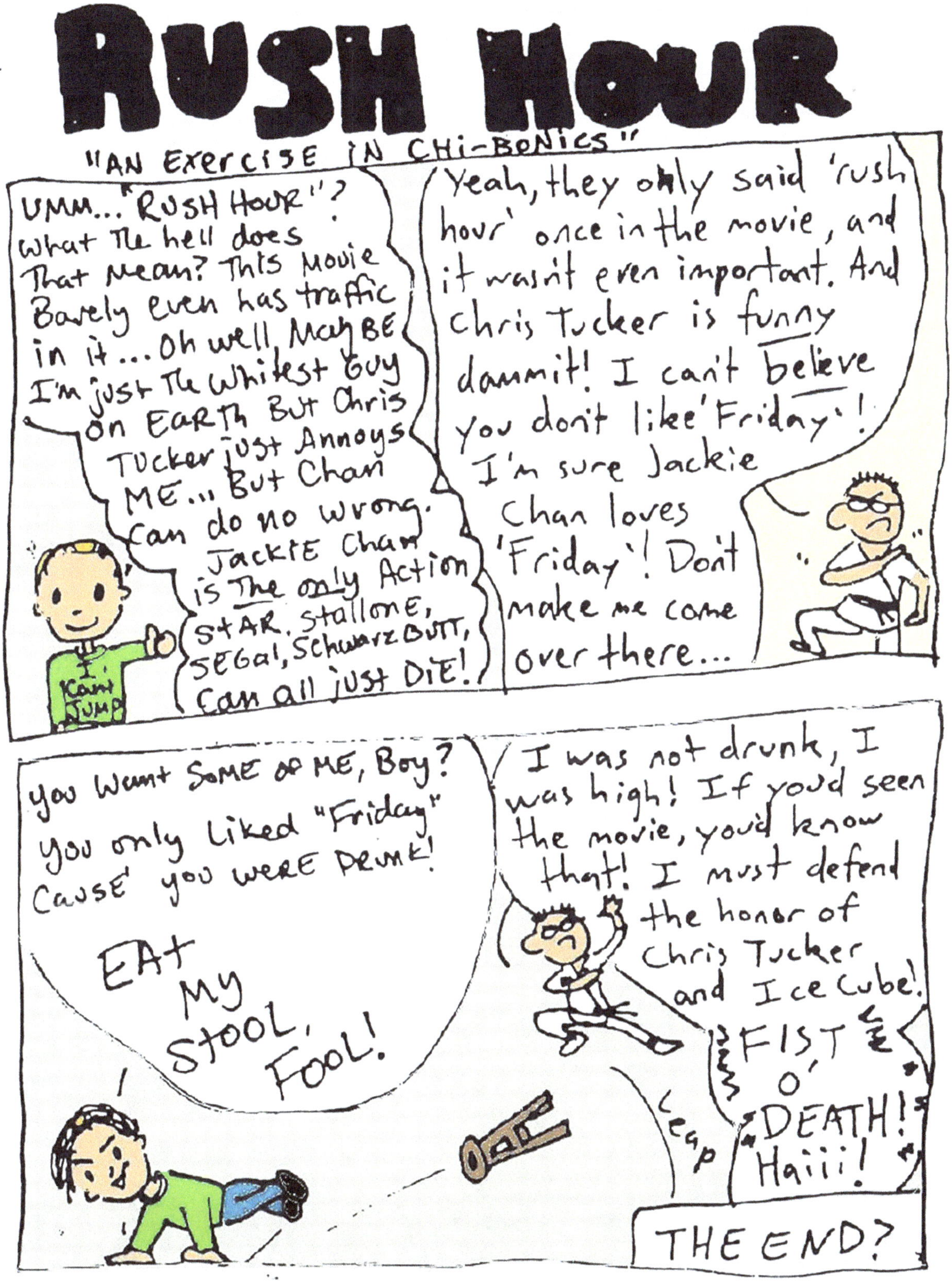
RUSH HOUR
"AN EXERCISE IN CHI-BONICS"
UMM... "RUSH HOUR"? What The hell does That Mean? This Movie Barely even has traffic in it... Oh well, MayBE I'm just The Whitest Guy on EARTH But Chris Tucker just Annoys ME... But Chan can do no wrong. JackiE Chan is The only Action StAR. Stallone, SEGal, SchwarzButt, can all just DiE!
I Kant Jump
Yeah, they only said 'rush hour' once in the movie, and it wasn't even important. And Chris Tucker is funny dammit! I can't believe you don't like 'Friday'! I'm sure Jackie Chan loves 'Friday'! Don't make me come over there...
You Want SOME OF ME, Boy? You only Liked "Friday" Cause' you WERE DRUNK!
EAT MY STOOL, FOOL!
I was not drunk, I was high! If you'd seen the movie, you'd know that! I must defend the honor of Chris Tucker and Ice Cube!
FIST O' DEATH! Haiii!
Leap
THE END?

FIRST COMIC EVER!

ACTION!!

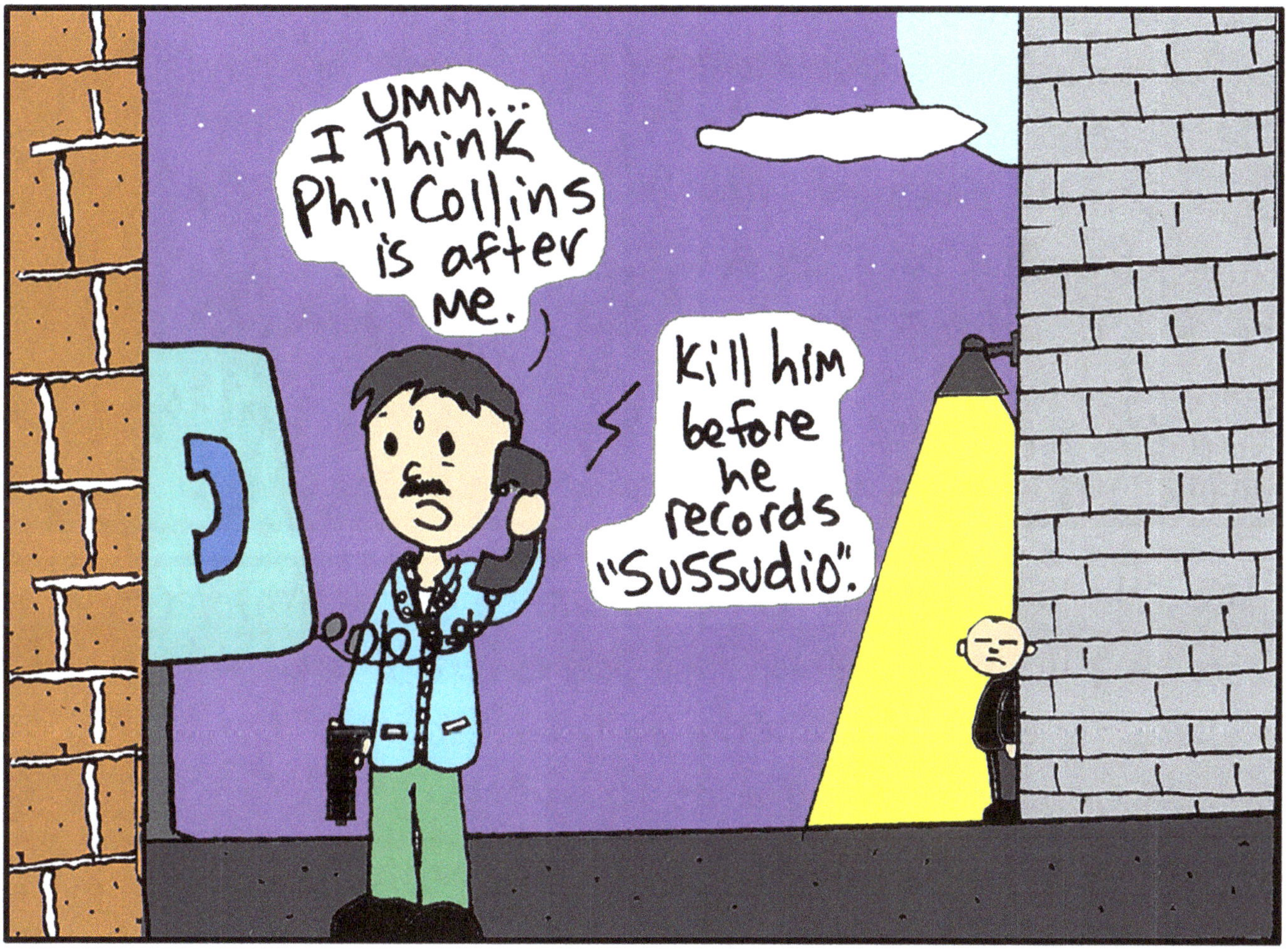
UMM...
I Think Phil Collins is after me.
Kill him before he records "Sussudio".

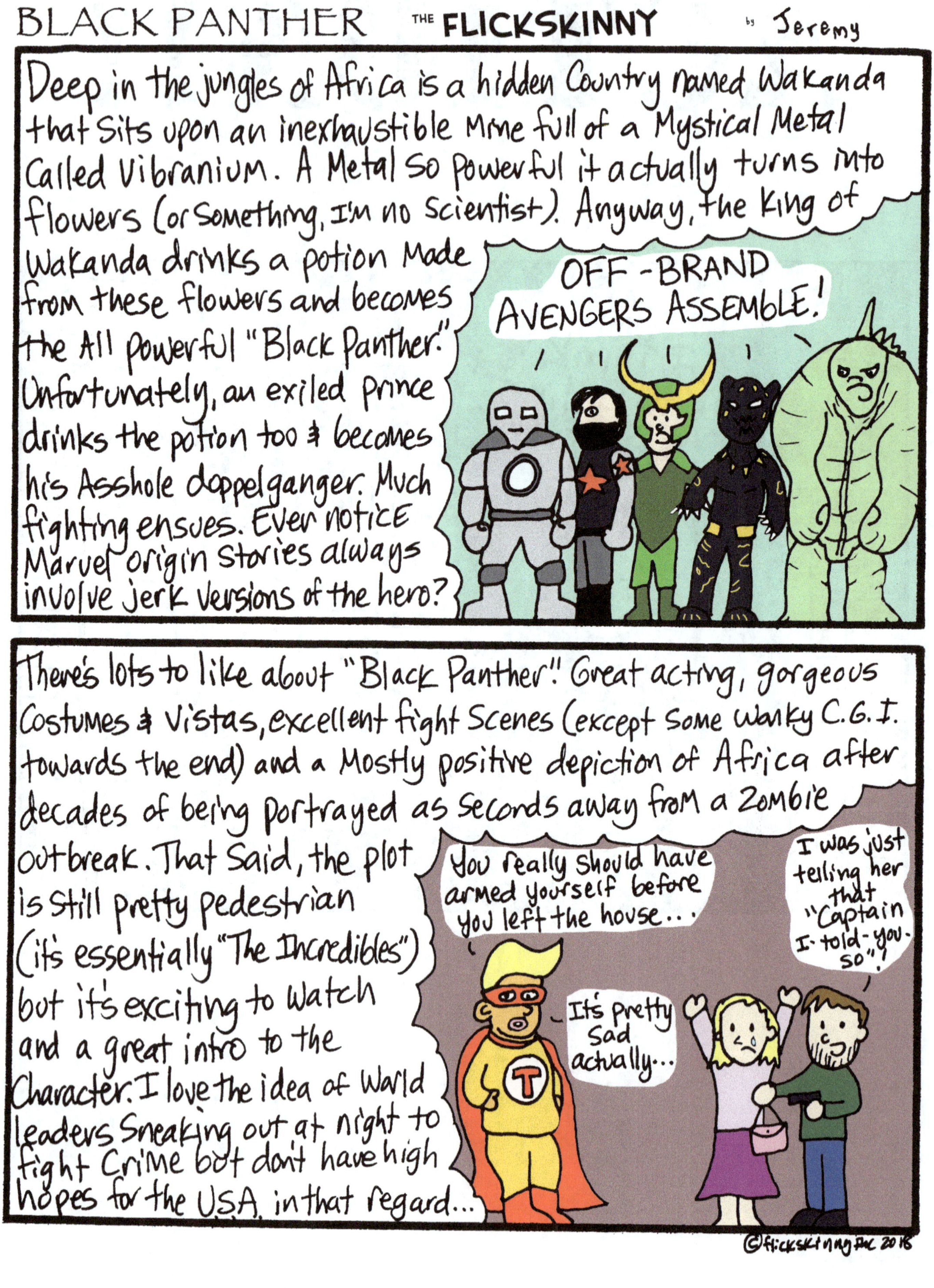
BLACK PANTHER
THE FLICKSKINNY
by Jeremy
Deep in the jungles of Africa is a hidden Country named Wakanda that Sits upon an inexhaustible Mine full of a Mystical Metal Called Vibranium. A Metal So powerful it actually turns into flowers (or Something, I'm no Scientist). Anyway, the King of Wakanda drinks a potion Made from these flowers and becomes the All powerful "Black Panther." Unfortunately, an exiled prince drinks the potion too & becomes his Asshole doppelganger. Much fighting ensues. Ever notice Marvel origin Stories always involve jerk versions of the hero?
OFF-BRAND AVENGERS ASSEMBLE!
There's lots to like about "Black Panther." Great acting, gorgeous Costumes & Vistas, excellent fight Scenes (except Some wanky C.G.I. towards the end) and a Mostly positive depiction of Africa after decades of being portrayed as seconds away from a Zombie outbreak. That Said, the plot is Still pretty pedestrian (it's essentially "The Incredibles") but it's exciting to watch and a great intro to the Character. I love the idea of World leaders Sneaking out at night to fight Crime but don't have high hopes for the USA in that regard...
You really should have armed yourself before you left the house...
It's pretty sad actually...
I was just telling her that "Captain I-told-you-so"!
T
©flickskinny inc 2018

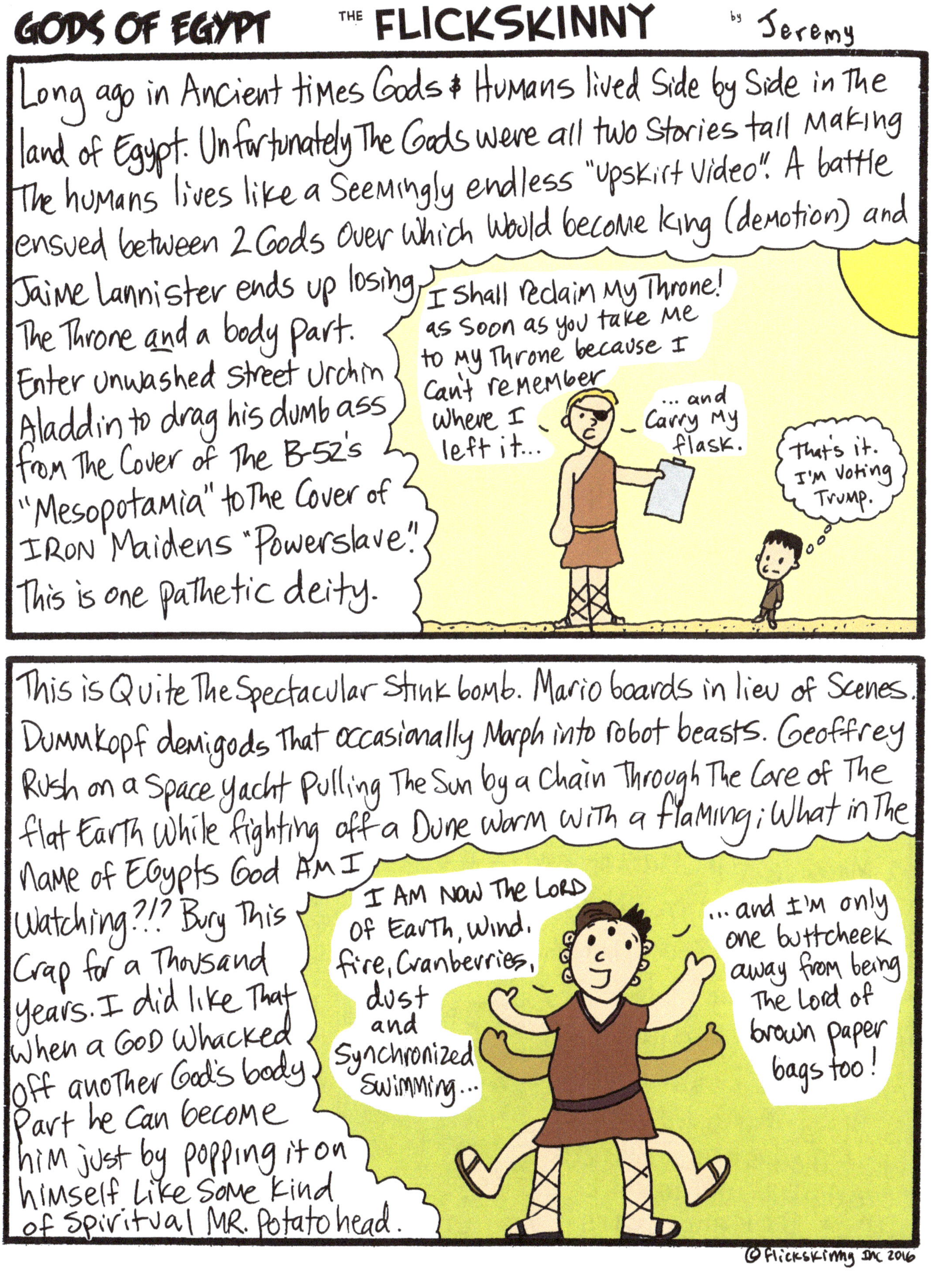
GODS OF EGYPT
THE FLICKSKINNY
by Jeremy
Long ago in Ancient times Gods & Humans lived Side by Side in The land of Egypt. Unfortunately The Gods were all two Stories tall Making The humans lives like a Seemingly endless "upskirt Video". A battle ensued between 2 Gods Over Which Would become King (demotion) and Jaime Lannister ends up losing The Throne and a body part. Enter unwashed street urchin Aladdin to drag his dumb ass from The Cover of The B-52's "Mesopotamia" to The Cover of IRON Maidens "Powerslave". This is one pathetic deity.
I Shall reclaim My Throne! as soon as you take Me to My Throne because I can't remember where I left it...
... and Carry My flask.
That's it. I'm Voting Trump.
This is Quite The Spectacular Stink bomb. Mario boards in lieu of Scenes. Dummkopf demigods That occasionally Morph into robot beasts. Geoffrey Rush on a Space yacht Pulling The Sun by a Chain Through The Core of The flat Earth while fighting off a Dune worm with a flaming; What in The name of Egypts God AM I Watching?!? Bury This Crap for a Thousand years. I did like That when a GOD Whacked off another God's body Part he can become him just by popping it on himself Like Some kind of Spiritual MR. Potato head.
I AM Now The LORD of Earth, Wind, fire, Cranberries, dust and Synchronized Swimming...
... and I'm only one buttcheek away from being The Lord of brown paper bags too!
© Flickskinny Inc 2016

THE GREAT WALL

THE FLICKSKINNY by Jeremy

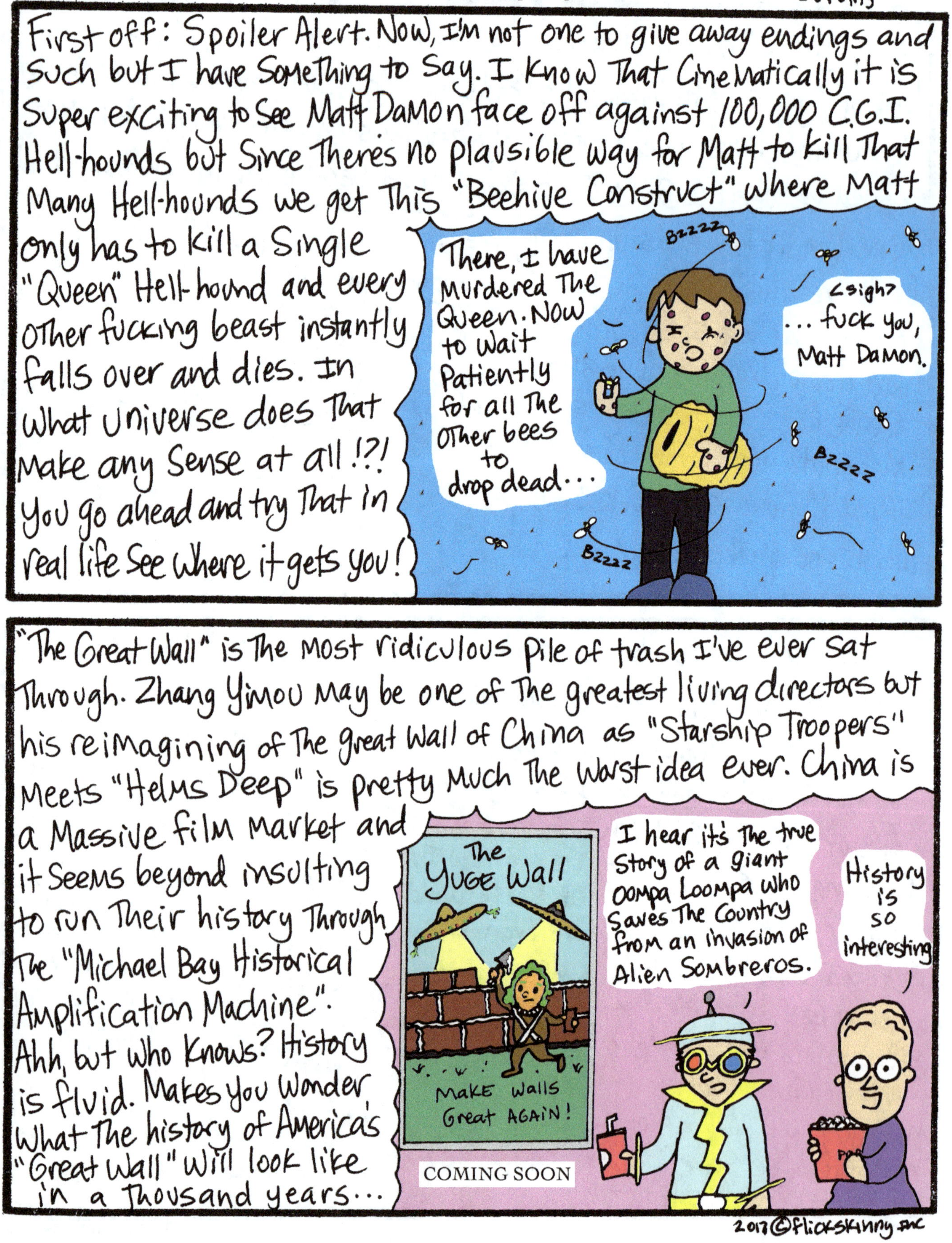

First off: Spoiler Alert. Now, I'm not one to give away endings and Such but I have Something to Say. I know That CineMatically it is Super exciting to See Matt DaMon face off against 100,000 C.G.I. Hell-hounds but Since Theres no plausible way for Matt to kill That Many Hell-hounds we get This "Beehive Construct" where Matt only has to kill a Single "Queen" Hell-hound and every Other fucking beast instantly falls over and dies. In What universe does That Make any Sense at all!?! You go ahead and try That in real life See where it gets you!
There, I have Murdered The Queen. Now to Wait Patiently for all The Other bees to drop dead...
Bzzzz
<sigh> ... fuck you, Matt DaMon.
Bzzzz
Bzzzz
"The Great Wall" is The Most ridiculous pile of trash I've ever sat Through. Zhang Yimou May be one of The greatest living directors but his reiMagining of The great Wall of China as "Starship Troopers" Meets "HelMs Deep" is pretty Much The Worst idea ever. China is a Massive film Market and it Seems beyond insulting to run Their history Through The "Michael Bay Historical Amplification Machine". Ahh, but who Knows? History is fluid. Makes you Wonder What The history of America's "Great Wall" Will look like in a Thousand years...
The Yuge Wall
Make Walls Great AGAIN!
COMING SOON
I hear it's The true Story of a giant OOMpa LooMpa who Saves The Country from an invasion of Alien SoMbreros.
History is so interesting

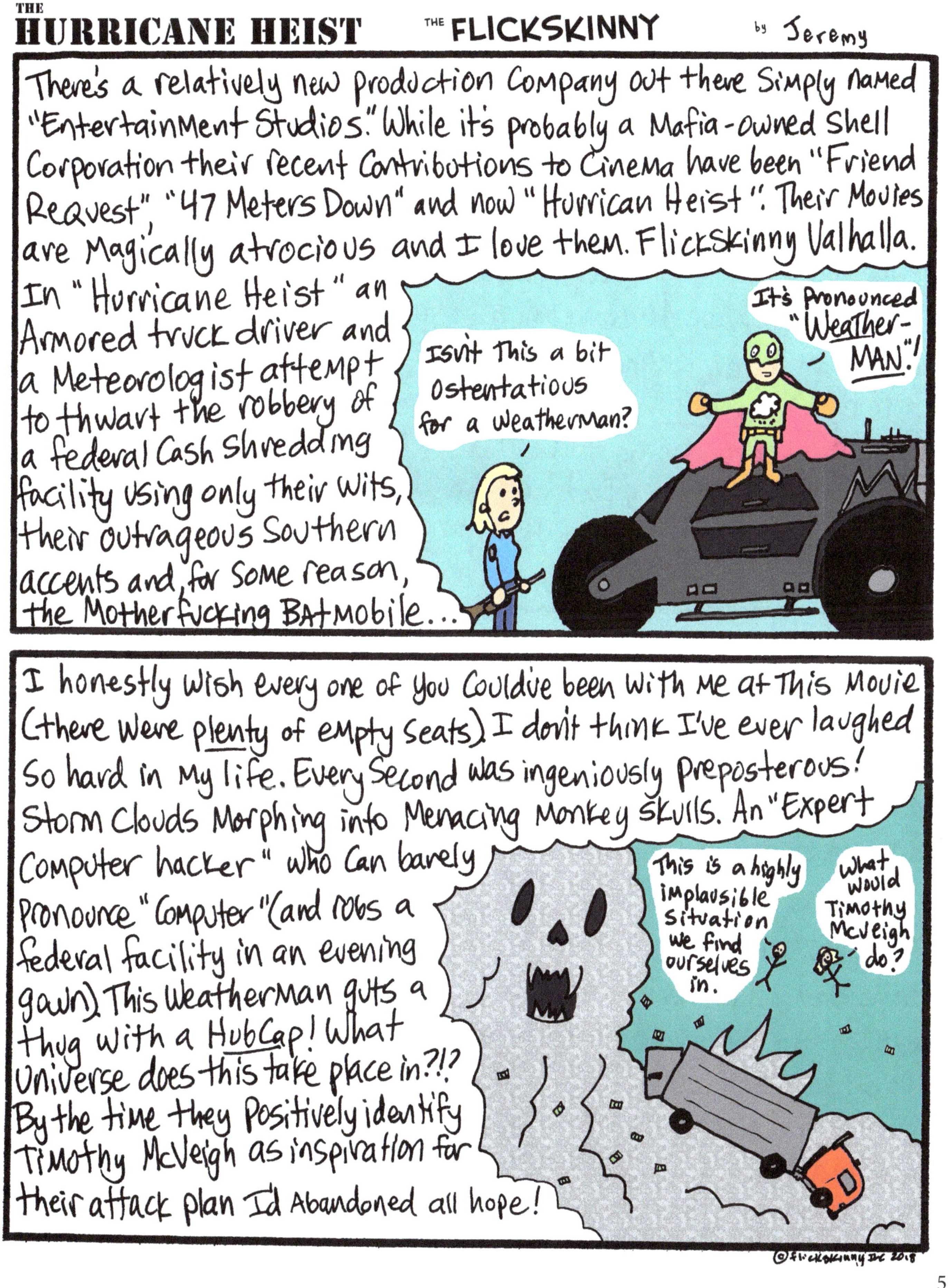
THE HURRICANE HEIST
THE FLICKSKINNY
by Jeremy
There's a relatively new production Company out there Simply named "Entertainment Studios." While it's probably a Mafia-owned Shell Corporation their recent Contributions to Cinema have been "Friend Request", "47 Meters Down" and now "Hurrican Heist". Their Movies are Magically atrocious and I love them. FlickSkinny Valhalla.
In "Hurricane Heist" an Armored truck driver and a Meteorologist attempt to thwart the robbery of a federal Cash shredding facility using only their wits, their outrageous Southern accents and, for some reason, the Motherfucking BATMobile...
Isn't this a bit ostentatious for a weatherman?
It's pronounced "Weather-MAN"!
I honestly wish every one of you Could've been with me at this Movie (there were plenty of empty seats) I don't think I've ever laughed so hard in my life. Every Second was ingeniously preposterous! Storm Clouds Morphing into Menacing Monkey Skulls. An "Expert Computer hacker" who can barely pronounce "Computer" (and robs a federal facility in an evening gown) This Weatherman guts a thug with a HubCap! What Universe does this take place in?!? By the time they Positively identify Timothy McVeigh as inspiration for their attack plan I'd Abandoned all hope!
This is a highly implausible situation we find ourselves in.
What would Timothy McVeigh do?
©FlickSkinny Inc 2018

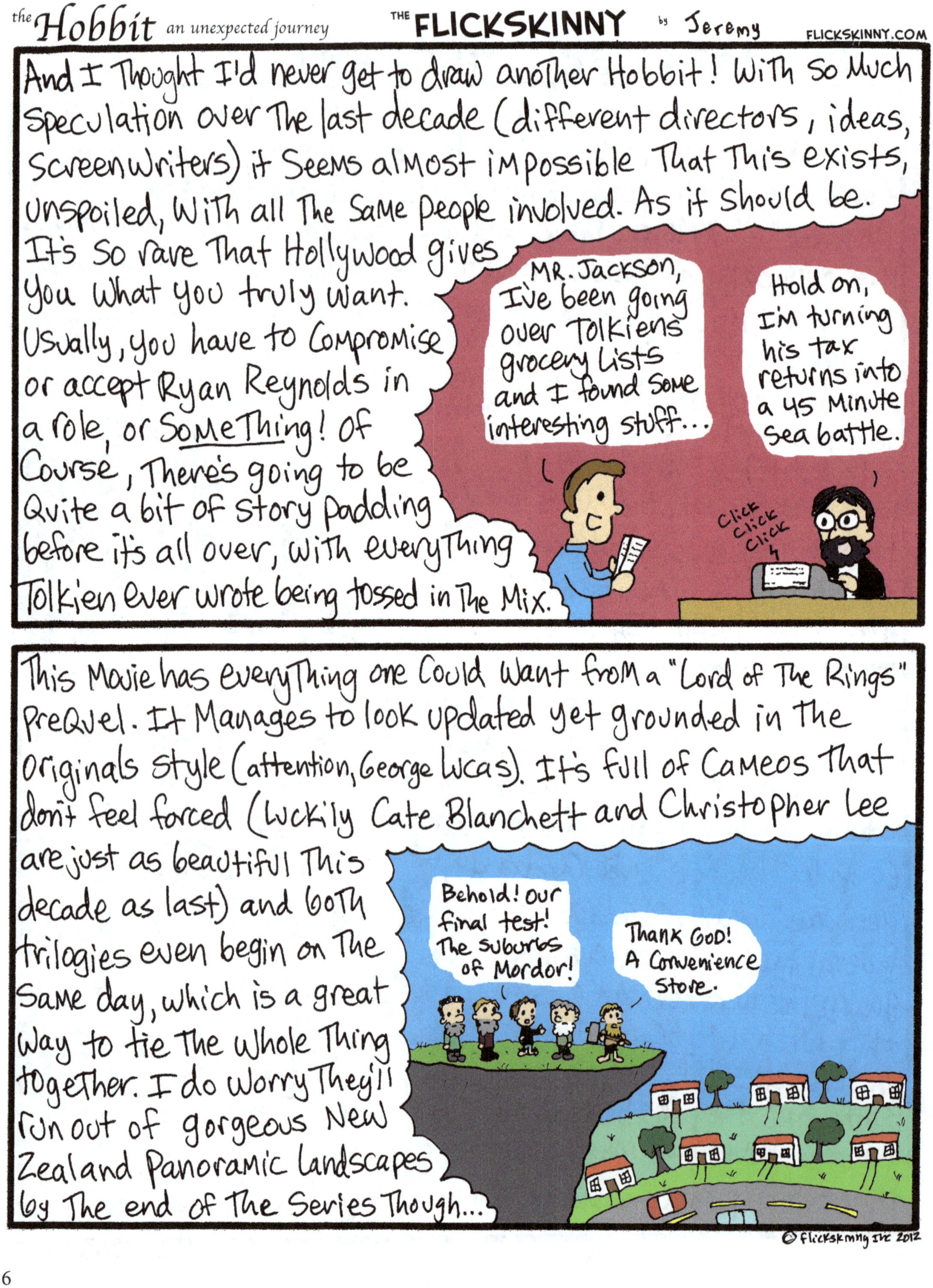
the Hobbit an unexpected journey
THE FLICKSKINNY by Jeremy
FLICKSKINNY.COM
And I Thought I'd never get to draw another Hobbit! With So Much Speculation over The last decade (different directors, ideas, Screenwriters) it Seems almost impossible That This exists, unspoiled, With all The Same people involved. As it Should be. It's So rare That Hollywood gives you what you truly want. Usually, you have to Compromise or accept Ryan Reynolds in a role, or SomeThing! Of Course, There's going to be Quite a bit of Story padding before it's all over, with everyThing Tolkien ever wrote being tossed in The Mix.
Mr. Jackson, I've been going over Tolkiens grocery Lists and I found Some interesting stuff...
Hold on, I'm turning his tax returns into a 45 Minute Sea battle.
Click Click Click
This Movie has everyThing one Could Want from a "Lord of The Rings" PreQuel. It Manages to look updated yet grounded in The Originals Style (attention, George Lucas). It's full of Cameos That don't feel forced (Luckily Cate Blanchett and Christopher Lee are just as beautiful This decade as last) and both trilogies even begin on The Same day, which is a great Way to tie The Whole Thing together. I do Worry They'll run out of gorgeous New Zealand Panoramic landscapes by The end of The Series Though...
Behold! Our final test! The suburbs of Mordor!
Thank God! A Convenience Store.
© Flickskinny Inc 2012

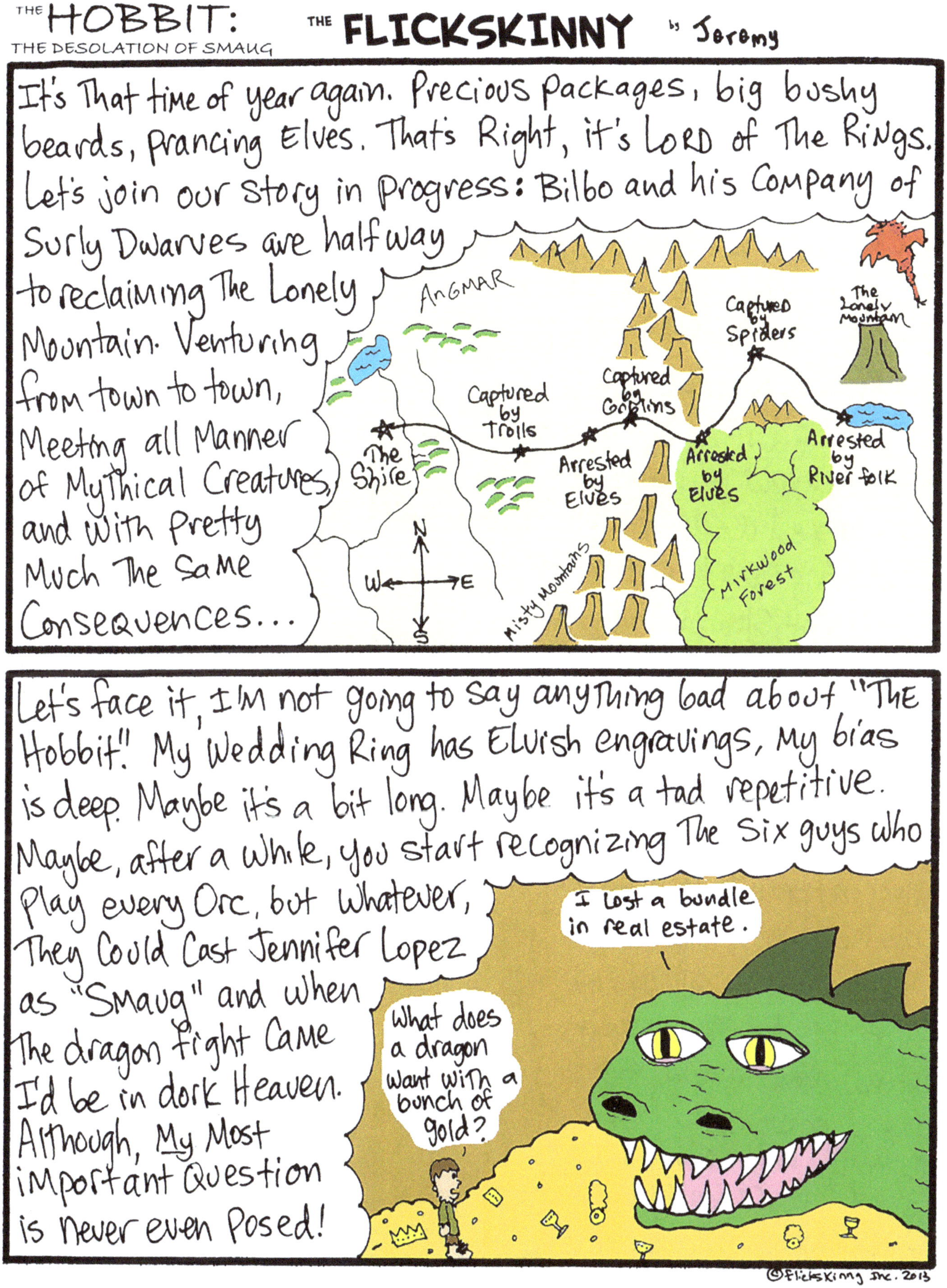
THE HOBBIT: THE DESOLATION OF SMAUG
THE FLICKSKINNY by Jeremy
It's That time of year again. Precious packages, big bushy beards, prancing Elves. That's Right, it's LORD of The Rings. Let's join our Story in progress: Bilbo and his Company of Surly Dwarves are halfway to reclaiming The Lonely Mountain. Venturing from town to town, Meeting all Manner of Mythical Creatures, and with Pretty Much The SaMe Consequences...
AnGMAR
The Shire
Captured by Trolls
Arrested by Elves
Captured by Goblins
Misty Mountains
Arrested by Elves
Captured by Spiders
Mirkwood Forest
Arrested by River folk
The Lonely Mountain
N
W
E
S
Let's face it, I'M not going to say anything bad about "The Hobbit." My Wedding Ring has Elvish engravings, My bias is deep. Maybe it's a bit long. Maybe it's a tad repetitive. Maybe, after a while, you start recognizing The Six guys who Play every Orc, but whatever, They Could Cast Jennifer Lopez as "Smaug" and when The dragon fight Came I'd be in dork Heaven. Although, My Most important Question is never even Posed!
I Lost a bundle in real estate.
What does a dragon want with a bunch of gold?
©FlickSkinny Inc. 2013

King Arthur:
Legend of the Sword (2017)

THE FLICKSKINNY by Jeremy

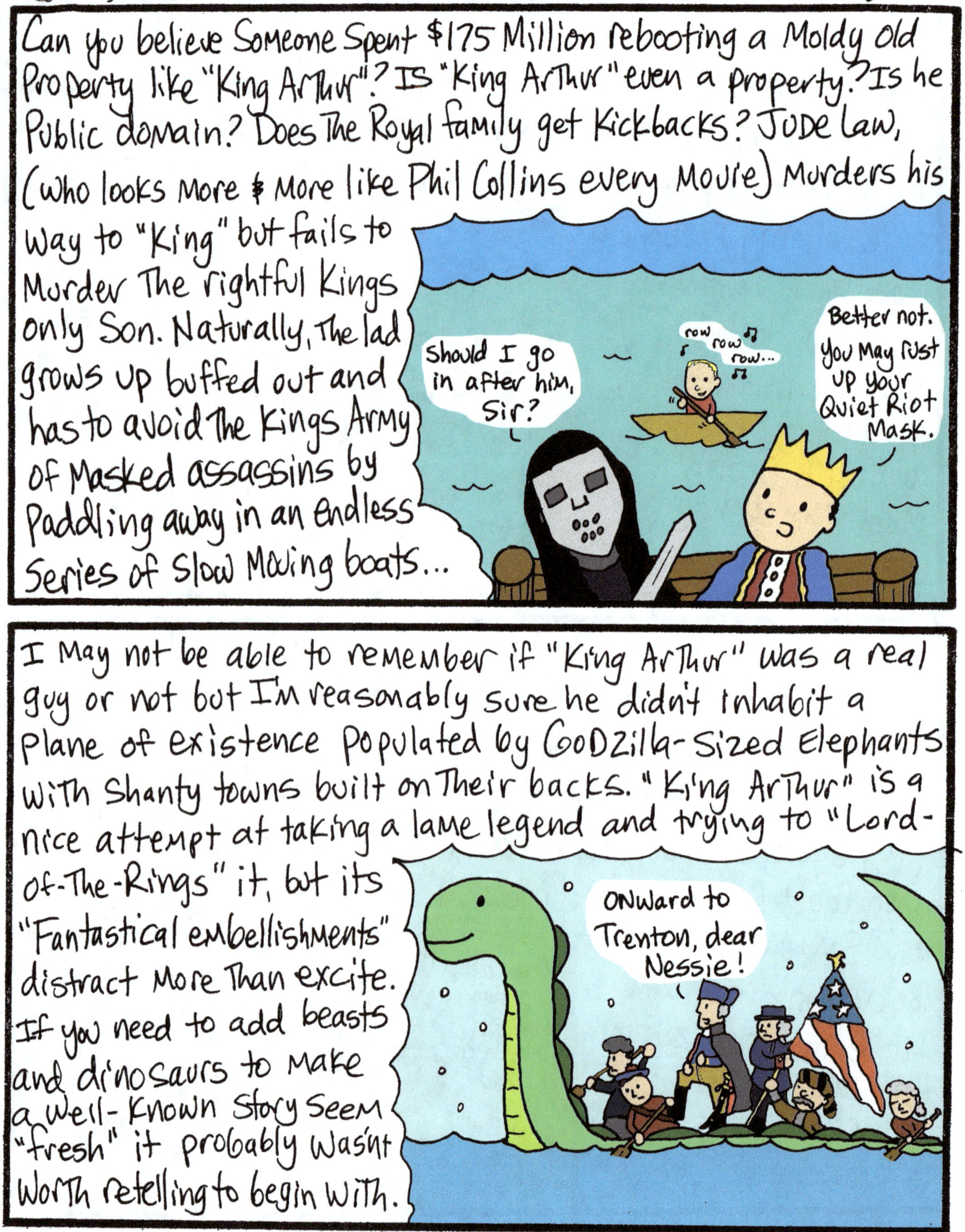
Can you believe Someone Spent $175 Million rebooting a Moldy old Property like "King Arthur"? Is "King Arthur" even a property? Is he Public domain? Does The Royal family get Kickbacks? JUDE Law, (who looks More & More like Phil Collins every Movie) Murders his way to "King" but fails to Murder The rightful Kings only Son. Naturally, The lad grows up buffed out and has to avoid The Kings Army of Masked assassins by Paddling away in an endless Series of Slow Moving boats...
Should I go in after him, Sir?
row row row...
Better not. You May rust up your Quiet Riot Mask.
I May not be able to remember if "King Arthur" was a real guy or not but I'm reasonably sure he didn't inhabit a Plane of existence populated by GoDZilla-Sized Elephants with Shanty towns built on Their backs. "King Arthur" is a nice attempt at taking a lame legend and trying to "Lord-of-The-Rings" it, but its "Fantastical embellishments" distract More Than excite. If you need to add beasts and dinosaurs to Make a Well-Known Story Seem "fresh" it probably wasn't worth retelling to begin with.
ONward to Trenton, dear Nessie!

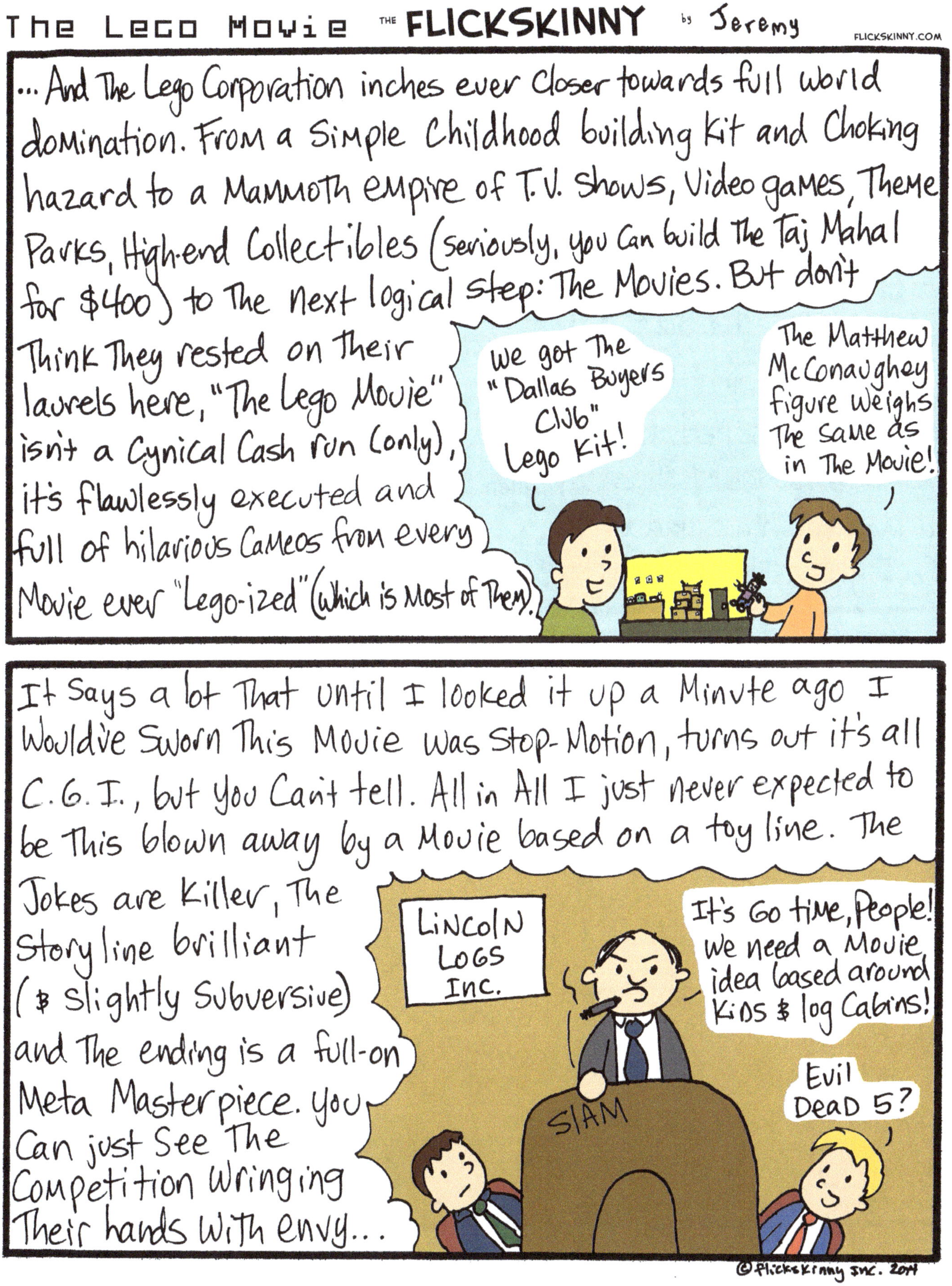
The Lego Movie
THE FLICKSKINNY by Jeremy
FLICKSKINNY.COM
...And The Lego Corporation inches ever closer towards full world domination. From a simple childhood building kit and choking hazard to a mammoth empire of T.V. shows, video games, theme parks, high-end collectibles (seriously, you can build the Taj Mahal for $400) to the next logical step: The Movies. But don't think they rested on their laurels here, "The Lego Movie" isn't a cynical cash run (only), it's flawlessly executed and full of hilarious cameos from every movie ever "Lego-ized" (which is most of them).
We got the "Dallas Buyers Club" Lego kit!
The Matthew McConaughey figure weighs the same as in the movie!
It says a lot that until I looked it up a minute ago I would've sworn this movie was stop-motion, turns out it's all C.G.I., but you can't tell. All in all I just never expected to be this blown away by a movie based on a toy line. The jokes are killer, the storyline brilliant ($ slightly subversive) and the ending is a full-on meta masterpiece. You can just see the competition wringing their hands with envy...
LINCOLN LOGS INC.
It's go time, people! We need a movie idea based around kids $ log cabins!
SIAM
Evil Dead 5?
© FlickSkinny Inc. 2014

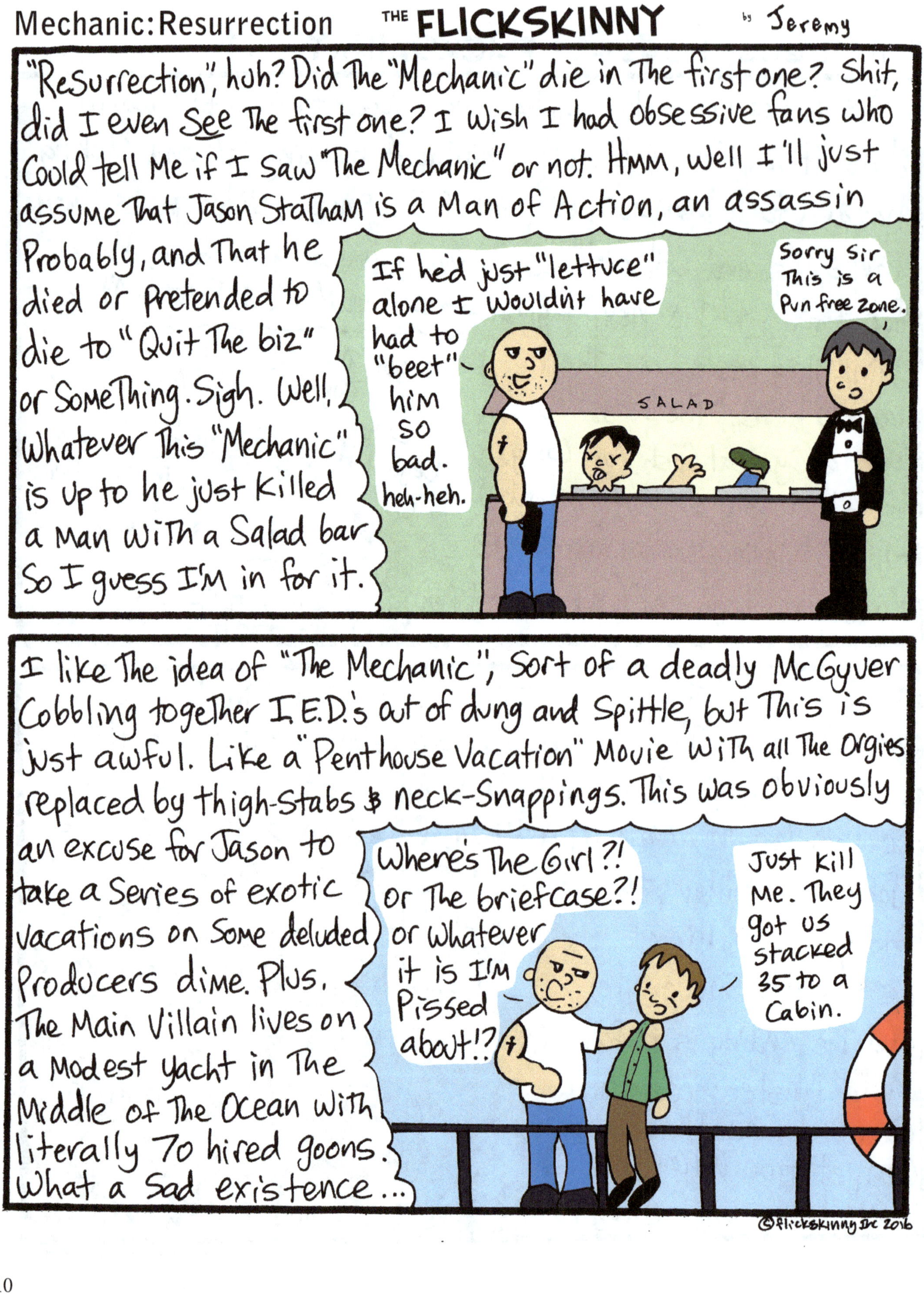
Mechanic: Resurrection
THE FLICKSKINNY
by Jeremy
"Resurrection", huh? Did The "Mechanic" die in The first one? Shit, did I even See The first one? I wish I had obsessive fans who Could tell Me if I saw "The Mechanic" or not. HMM, well I'll just assume That Jason Statham is a Man of Action, an assassin Probably, and That he died or Pretended to die to "Quit The biz" or SomeThing. Sigh. Well, Whatever This "Mechanic" is up to he just Killed a Man With a Salad bar So I guess I'M in for it.
If he'd just "lettuce" alone I wouldn't have had to "beet" him so bad. heh-heh.
SALAD
Sorry Sir This is a Pun free zone.
I like The idea of "The Mechanic", Sort of a deadly McGyver Cobbling together I.E.D.'s out of dung and Spittle, but This is just awful. Like a "Penthouse Vacation" Movie With all The Orgies replaced by thigh-Stabs & neck-Snappings. This was obviously an excuse for Jason to take a Series of exotic vacations on Some deluded Producers dime. Plus, The Main Villain lives on a Modest yacht in The Middle of The Ocean with literally 70 hired goons. What a Sad existence...
Where's The Girl?! or The briefcase?! or Whatever it is I'M Pissed about!?
Just Kill Me. They got us stacked 35 to a Cabin.
©flickskinny Inc 2016

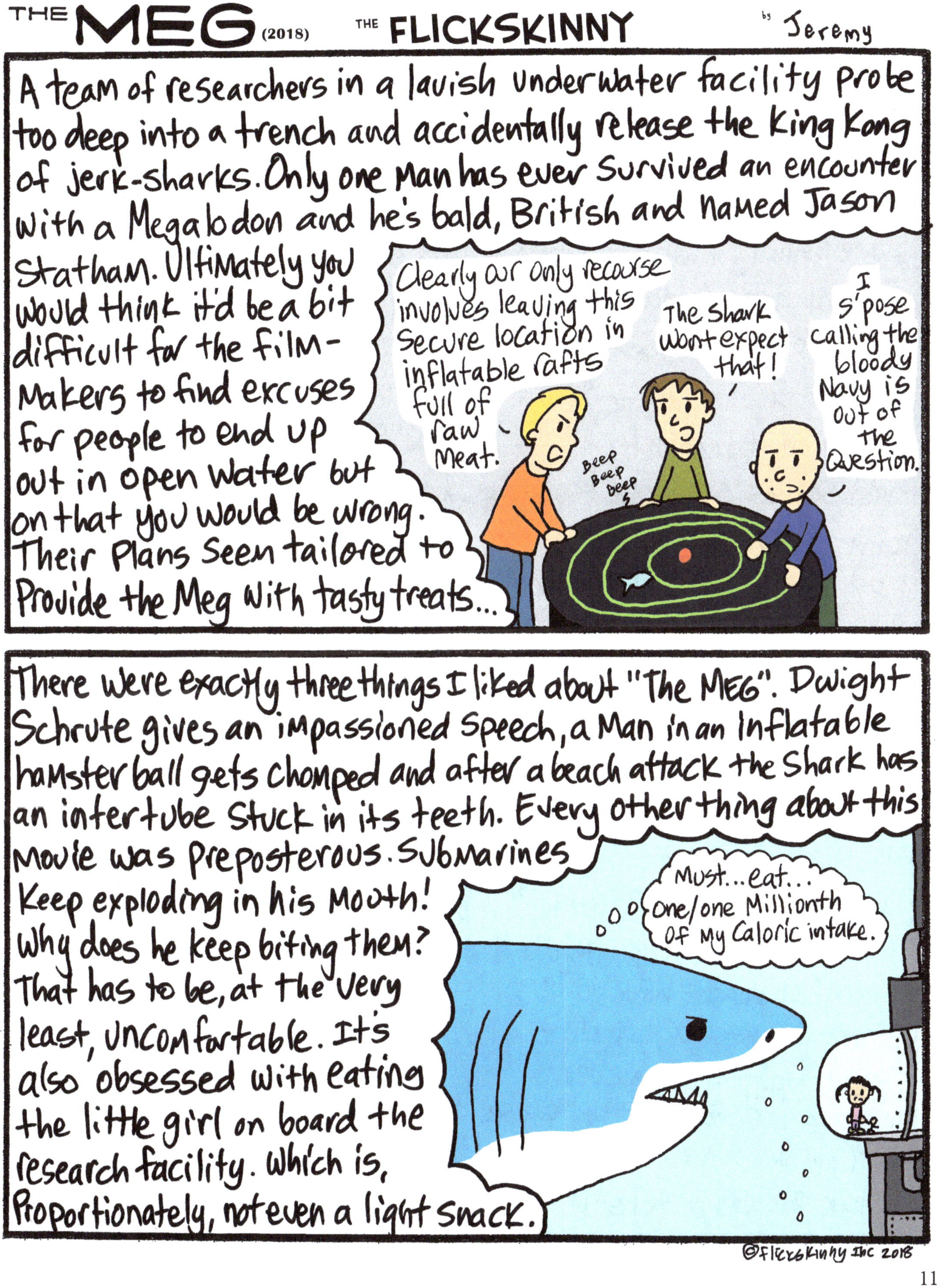
THE MEG (2018)
THE FLICKSKINNY
by Jeremy
A team of researchers in a lavish underwater facility probe too deep into a trench and accidentally release the King Kong of jerk-sharks. Only one man has ever survived an encounter with a Megalodon and he's bald, British and named Jason Statham. Ultimately you would think it'd be a bit difficult for the film-makers to find excuses for people to end up out in open water but on that you would be wrong. Their plans seem tailored to provide the Meg with tasty treats...
Clearly our only recourse involves leaving this secure location in inflatable rafts full of raw meat.
The shark won't expect that!
I s'pose calling the bloody Navy is out of the question.
Beep Beep Beep
There were exactly three things I liked about "The MEG". Dwight Schrute gives an impassioned speech, a man in an inflatable hamster ball gets chomped and after a beach attack the shark has an intertube stuck in its teeth. Every other thing about this movie was preposterous. Submarines keep exploding in his mouth! Why does he keep biting them? That has to be, at the very least, uncomfortable. It's also obsessed with eating the little girl on board the research facility. Which is, proportionately, not even a light snack.
Must...eat... one/one millionth of my caloric intake.
©FlickSkinny Inc 2018

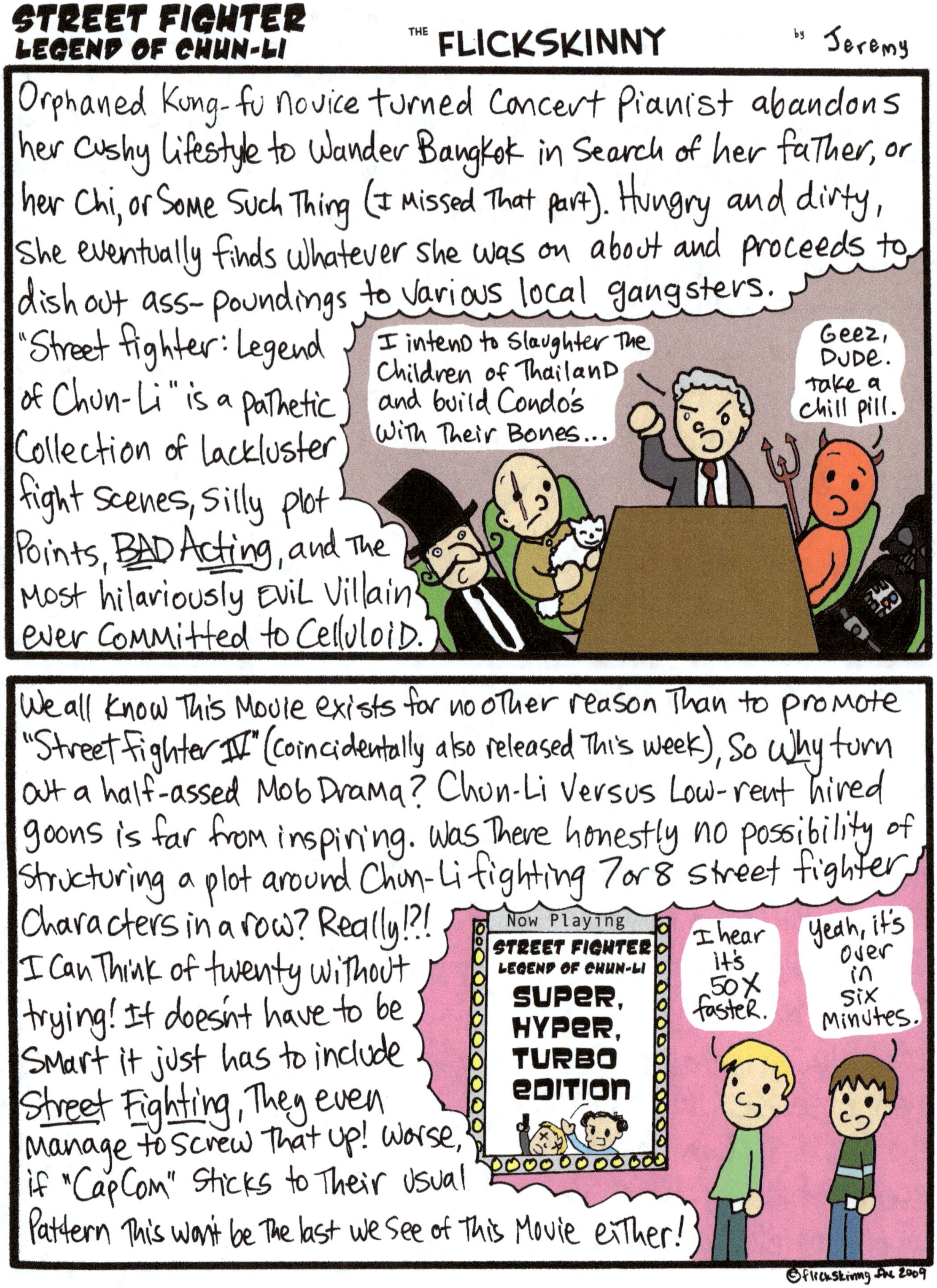

STREET FIGHTER
LEGEND OF CHUN-LI
THE FLICKSKINNY
by Jeremy
Orphaned Kung-fu novice turned Concert Pianist abandons her Cushy lifestyle to Wander Bangkok in Search of her father, or her Chi, or Some Such Thing (I Missed That part). Hungry and dirty, She eventually finds whatever She was on about and proceeds to dish out ass-poundings to various local gangsters.
"Street fighter: Legend of Chun-Li" is a paThetic Collection of lackluster fight scenes, silly plot Points, BAD Acting, and The Most hilariously EViL Villain ever COMMitted to CelluloiD.
I intenD to Slaughter The Children of ThailanD and build Condo's With Their Bones...
Geez, DuDe. Take a chill pill.
We all know This Movie exists for no other reason Than to promote "Street Fighter IV" (coincidentally also released This week), So Why turn out a half-assed Mob Drama? Chun-Li Versus Low-rent hired goons is far from inspiring. Was There honestly no possibility of Structuring a plot around Chun-Li fighting 7 or 8 street fighter Characters in a row? Really!?! I Can Think of twenty without trying! It doesn't have to be Smart it just has to include Street Fighting, They even manage to Screw That up! Worse, if "CapCom" Sticks to Their usual Pattern This won't be The last we See of This Movie either!
Now Playing
STREET FIGHTER
LEGEND OF CHUN-LI
SUPER, HYPER, TURBO EDITION
I hear it's 50X faster.
Yeah, it's over in six minutes.
©flickskinny 2009

Tomb Raider THE FLICKSKINNY by Jeremy

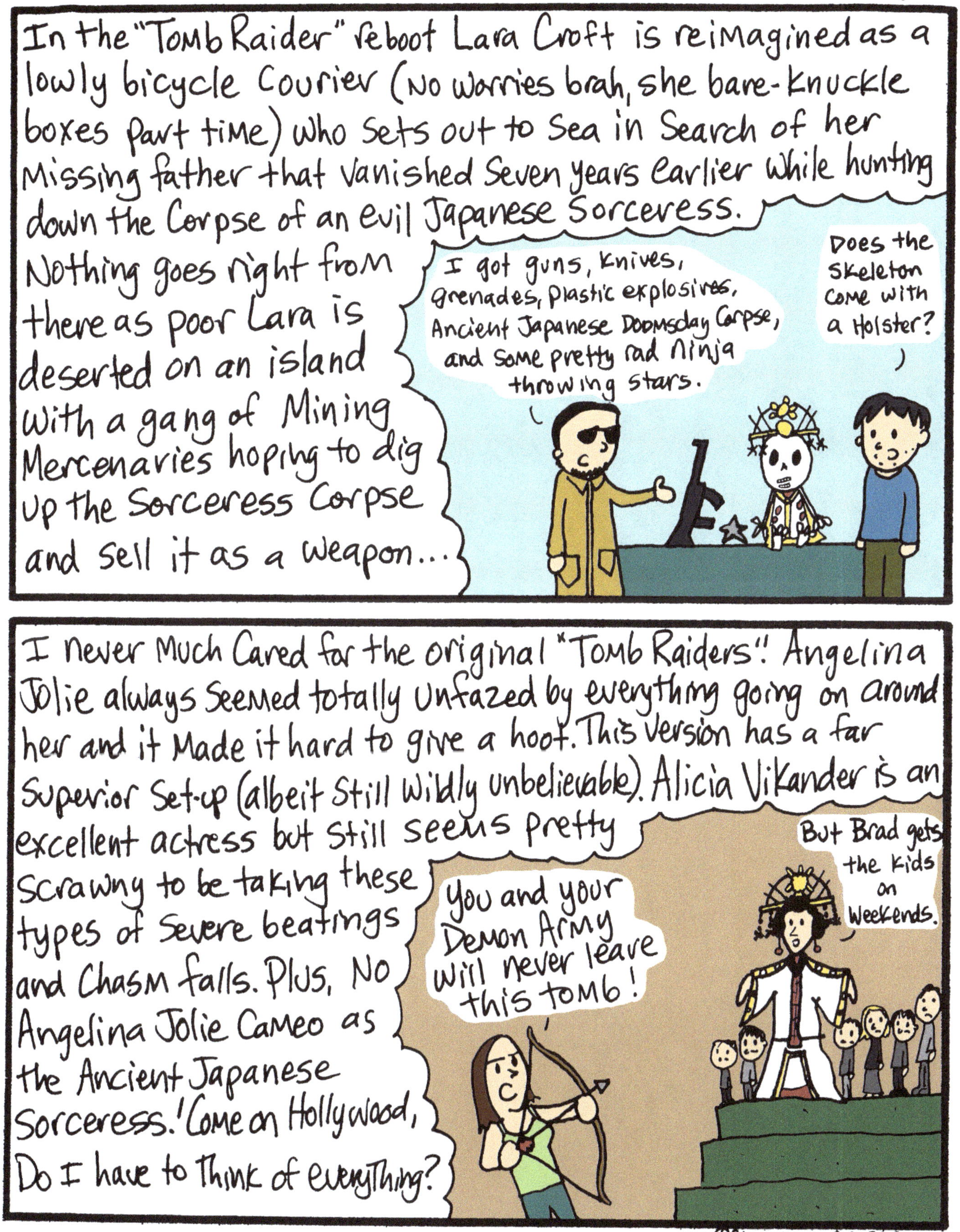
In the "Tomb Raider" reboot Lara Croft is reimagined as a lowly bicycle courier (No worries brah, she bare-knuckle boxes part time) who sets out to sea in search of her missing father that vanished seven years earlier while hunting down the corpse of an evil Japanese Sorceress.
Nothing goes right from there as poor Lara is deserted on an island with a gang of Mining Mercenaries hoping to dig up the Sorceress Corpse and sell it as a weapon...
I got guns, knives, grenades, plastic explosives, Ancient Japanese Doomsday Corpse, and some pretty rad ninja throwing stars.
Does the skeleton come with a Holster?
I never much cared for the original "Tomb Raiders". Angelina Jolie always seemed totally unfazed by everything going on around her and it made it hard to give a hoot. This version has a far superior set-up (albeit still wildly unbelievable). Alicia Vikander is an excellent actress but still seems pretty scrawny to be taking these types of severe beatings and chasm falls. Plus, No Angelina Jolie Cameo as the Ancient Japanese Sorceress.' Come on Hollywood, Do I have to think of everything?
You and your Demon Army will never leave this tomb!
But Brad gets the kids on weekends.

Drama!

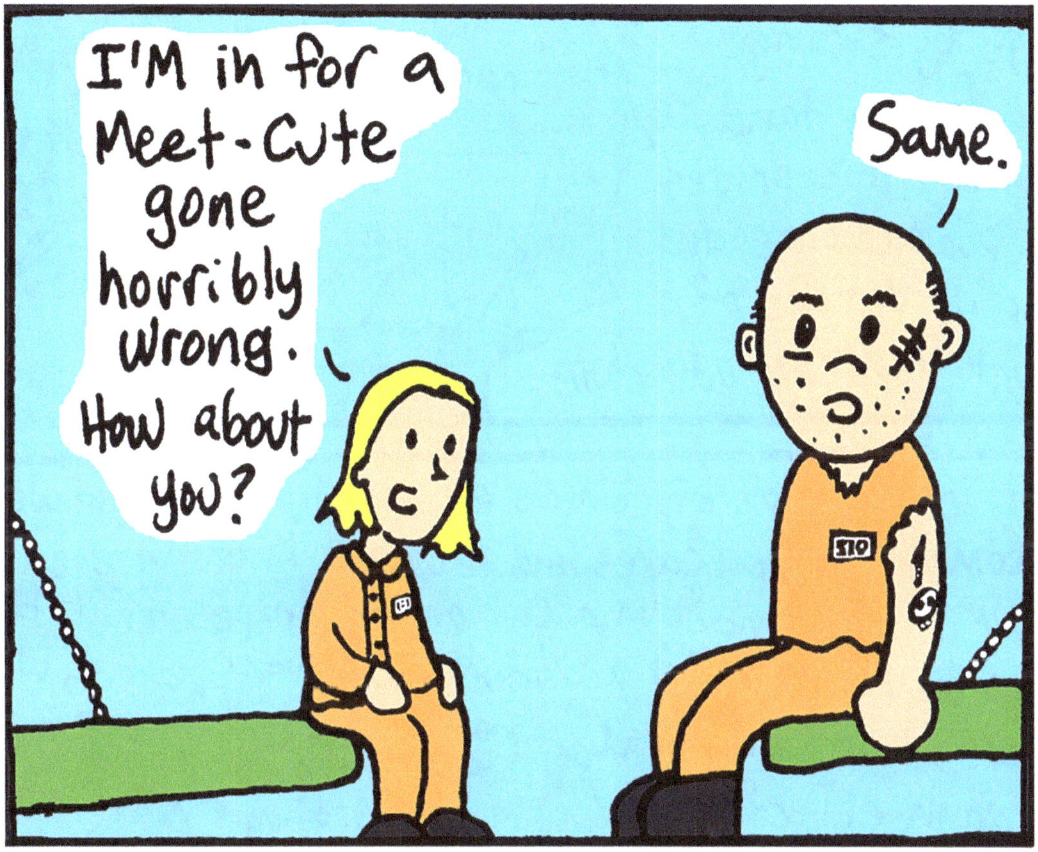
I'M in for a Meet-Cute gone horribly wrong. How about you?
Same.
510

47 Meters Down

THE FLICKSKINNY by Jeremy

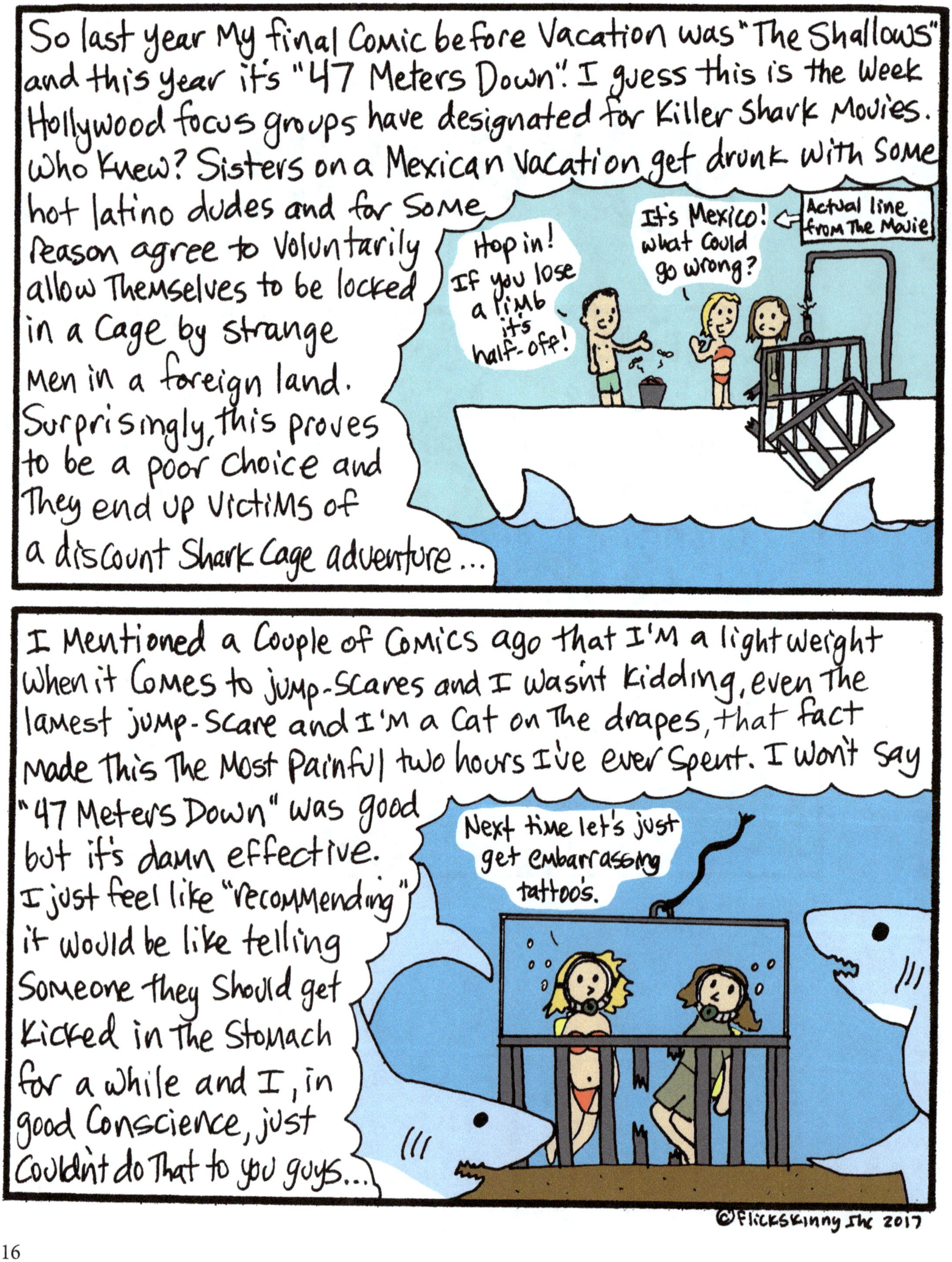
So last year My final Comic before Vacation was "The Shallows" and this year it's "47 Meters Down". I guess this is the Week Hollywood focus groups have designated for Killer Shark Movies. Who Knew? Sisters on a Mexican vacation get drunk with some hot latino dudes and for some reason agree to Voluntarily allow Themselves to be locked in a Cage by strange Men in a foreign land. Surprisingly, this proves to be a poor Choice and They end up Victims of a discount Shark Cage adventure...
Hop in! If you lose a limb it's half-off!
It's Mexico! what Could go wrong?
Actual line from The Movie
I Mentioned a Couple of Comics ago that I'M a lightweight when it Comes to jump-scares and I wasn't kidding, even the lamest jump-scare and I'M a Cat on The drapes, that fact Made This The Most Painful two hours I've ever Spent. I won't say "47 Meters Down" was good but it's damn effective. I just feel like "recommending" it would be like telling Someone they Should get Kicked in The Stomach for a while and I, in good Conscience, just Couldn't do That to you guys...
Next time let's just get embarrassing tattoo's.

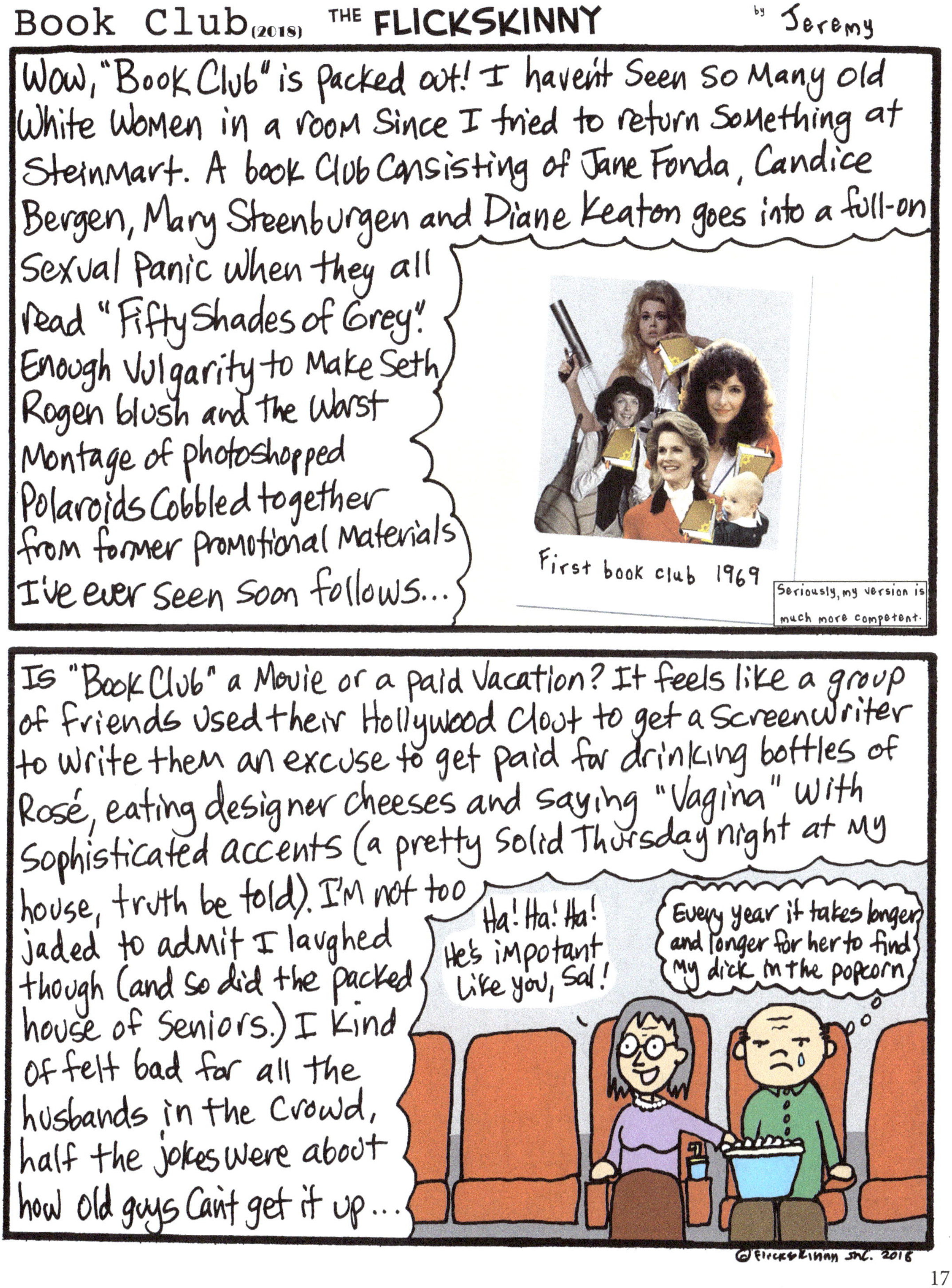
Book Club (2018) THE FLICKSKINNY by Jeremy
Wow, "Book Club" is packed out! I haven't seen so many old white women in a room since I tried to return something at SteinMart. A book club consisting of Jane Fonda, Candice Bergen, Mary Steenburgen and Diane Keaton goes into a full-on sexual panic when they all read "Fifty Shades of Grey". Enough vulgarity to make Seth Rogen blush and the worst montage of photoshopped polaroids cobbled together from former promotional materials I've ever seen soon follows...
First book club 1969
Seriously, my version is much more competent.
Is "Book Club" a movie or a paid vacation? It feels like a group of friends used their Hollywood clout to get a screenwriter to write them an excuse to get paid for drinking bottles of Rosé, eating designer cheeses and saying "Vagina" with sophisticated accents (a pretty solid Thursday night at my house, truth be told). I'm not too jaded to admit I laughed though (and so did the packed house of seniors.) I kind of felt bad for all the husbands in the crowd, half the jokes were about how old guys can't get it up...
Ha! Ha! Ha! He's impotant like you, Sal!
Every year it takes longer and longer for her to find my dick in the popcorn
©FlickSkinny Inc. 2018

50 Shades of Grey (2015) THE **FLICKSKINNY** by Jeremy

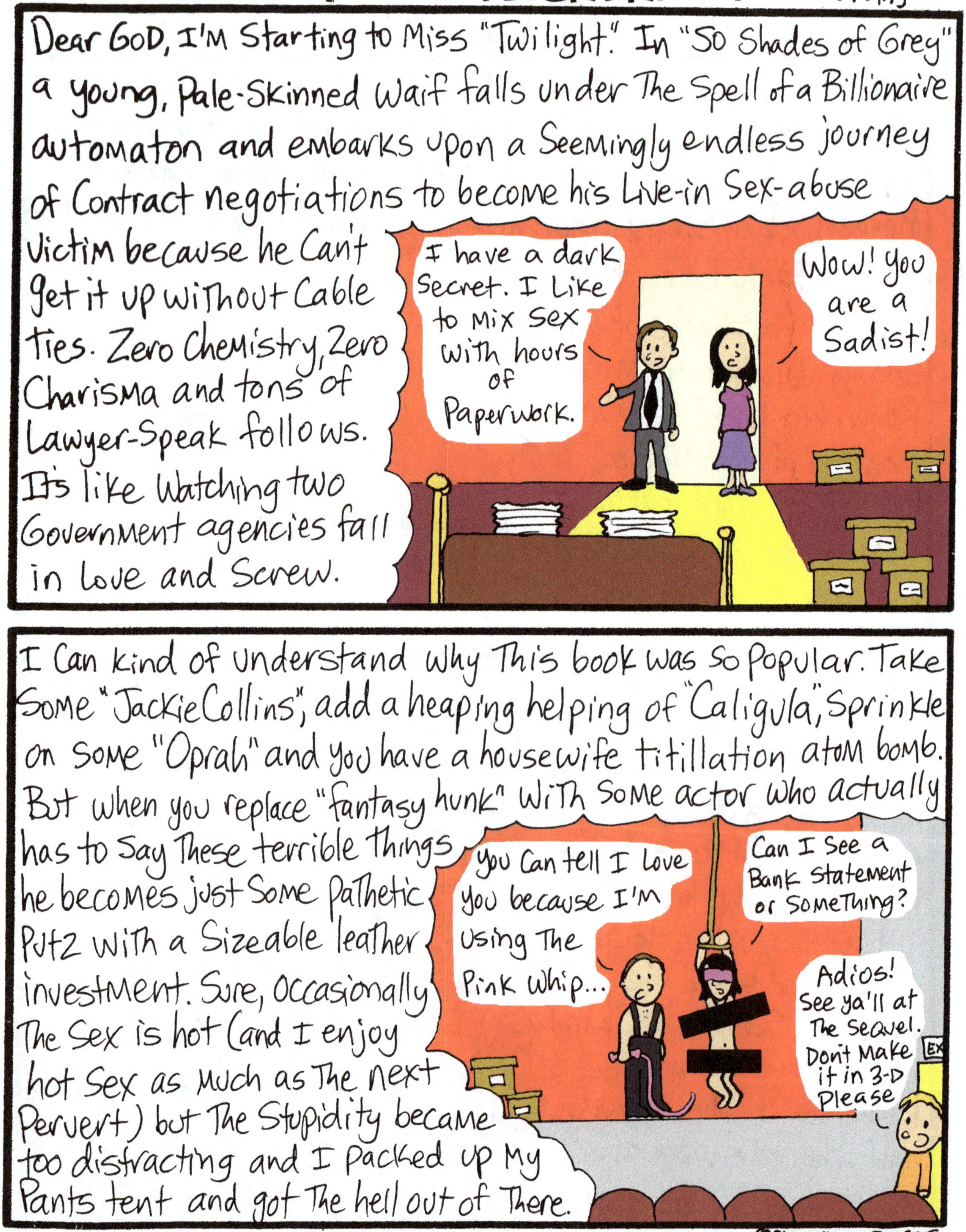
Dear GOD, I'M Starting to Miss "Twilight." In "50 Shades of Grey" a young, Pale-Skinned Waif falls under The Spell of a Billionaire automaton and embarks upon a Seemingly endless journey of Contract negotiations to become his Live-in Sex-abuse Victim because he Can't get it up without Cable ties. Zero Chemistry, Zero Charisma and tons of Lawyer-Speak follows. It's like Watching two Government agencies fall in love and Screw.
I have a dark Secret. I Like to Mix Sex with hours of Paperwork.
Wow! you are a Sadist!
I Can kind of understand why This book was so Popular. Take Some "Jackie Collins", add a heaping helping of "Caligula", Sprinkle on some "Oprah" and you have a housewife titillation atom bomb. But when you replace "fantasy hunk" With Some actor who actually has to Say These terrible things he becomes just Some pathetic Putz With a Sizeable leather investment. Sure, occasionally The Sex is hot (and I enjoy hot Sex as Much as The next Pervert) but The Stupidity became too distracting and I packed up My Pants tent and got The hell out of There.
You Can tell I Love You because I'M using The Pink whip...
Can I See a Bank Statement or SomeThing?
Adios! See ya'll at The Sequel. Don't Make it in 3-D Please

fifty shades darker (2017) THE FLICKSKINNY by Jeremy

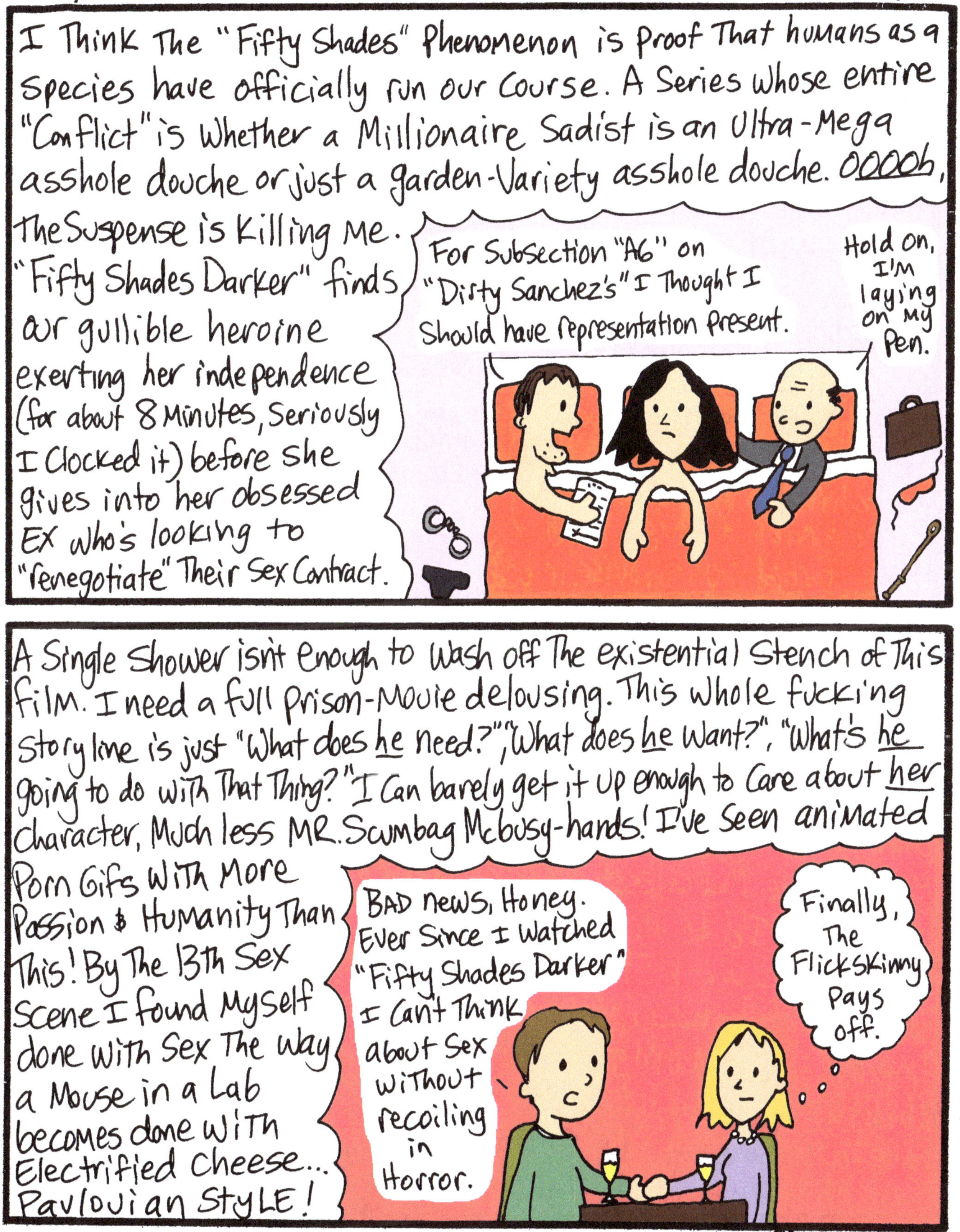
I Think The "Fifty Shades" Phenomenon is proof That humans as a species have officially run our course. A Series whose entire "Conflict" is Whether a Millionaire Sadist is an Ultra-Mega asshole douche or just a garden-Variety asshole douche. Ooooh, The Suspense is Killing Me.
"Fifty Shades Darker" finds our gullible heroine exerting her independence (for about 8 Minutes, Seriously I Clocked it) before she gives into her obsessed EX who's looking to "renegotiate" Their Sex Contract.
For Subsection "A6" on "Dirty Sanchez's" I Thought I Should have representation present.
Hold on, I'M laying on My Pen.
A Single Shower isn't enough to wash off The existential Stench of This film. I need a full prison-Movie delousing. This whole fucking Story line is just "What does he need?", "What does he Want?", "What's he going to do with That Thing?" I Can barely get it up enough to Care about her character, Much less MR. Scumbag Mcbusy-hands! I've Seen animated Porn Gifs With More Passion & Humanity Than This! By The 13th Sex Scene I found Myself done With Sex The way a Mouse in a Lab becomes done With Electrified Cheese... Pavlovian STyLE!
BAD news, Honey. Ever Since I watched "Fifty Shades Darker" I Can't Think about Sex without recoiling in Horror.
Finally, The FlickSkinny Pays off.

FIFTY SHADES FREED (2018) THE FLICKSKINNY by Jeremy

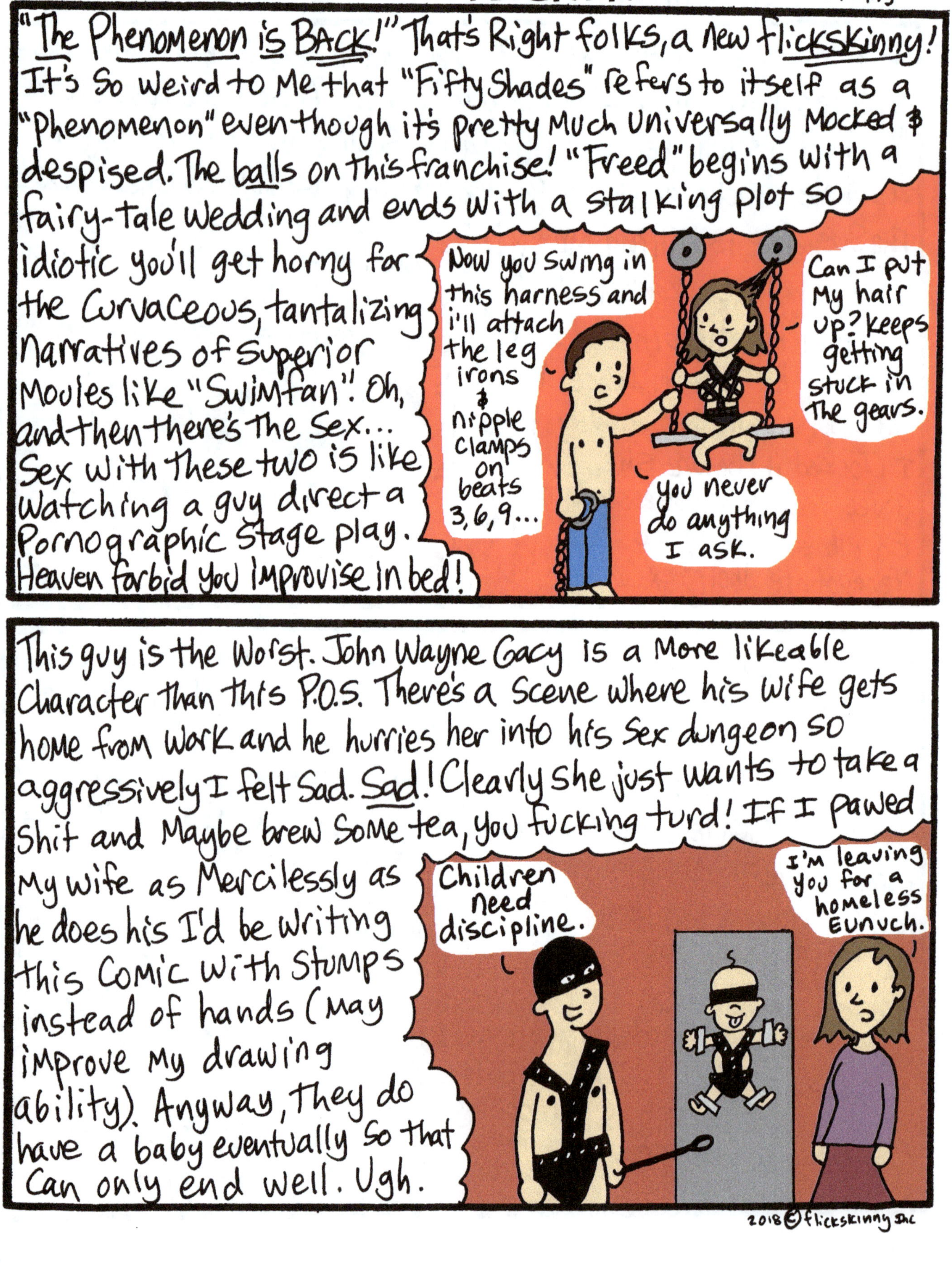

"The Phenomenon is BACK!" That's Right folks, a new flickSkinny! It's So Weird to Me that "Fifty Shades" refers to itself as a "phenomenon" even though it's pretty Much Universally Mocked $ despised. The balls on this franchise! "Freed" begins with a fairy-tale wedding and ends with a stalking plot so idiotic you'll get horny for the Curvaceous, tantalizing narratives of Superior Movies like "SwimFan". Oh, and then there's the Sex... Sex with these two is like Watching a guy direct a Pornographic Stage play. Heaven forbid you improvise in bed!
Now you swing in this harness and i'll attach the leg irons $ nipple clamps on beats 3, 6, 9...
Can I put My hair up? keeps getting stuck in the gears.
you never do anything I ask.
This guy is the Worst. John Wayne Gacy is a More likeable Character than this P.O.S. There's a Scene where his wife gets home from Work and he hurries her into his Sex dungeon so aggressively I felt Sad. Sad! Clearly she just wants to take a Shit and Maybe brew Some tea, you fucking turd! If I pawed My wife as Mercilessly as he does his I'd be writing this Comic with Stumps instead of hands (May improve My drawing ability). Anyway, they do have a baby eventually so that Can only end well. Ugh.
Children need discipline.
I'm leaving you for a homeless Eunuch.
2018 © flickskinny Inc

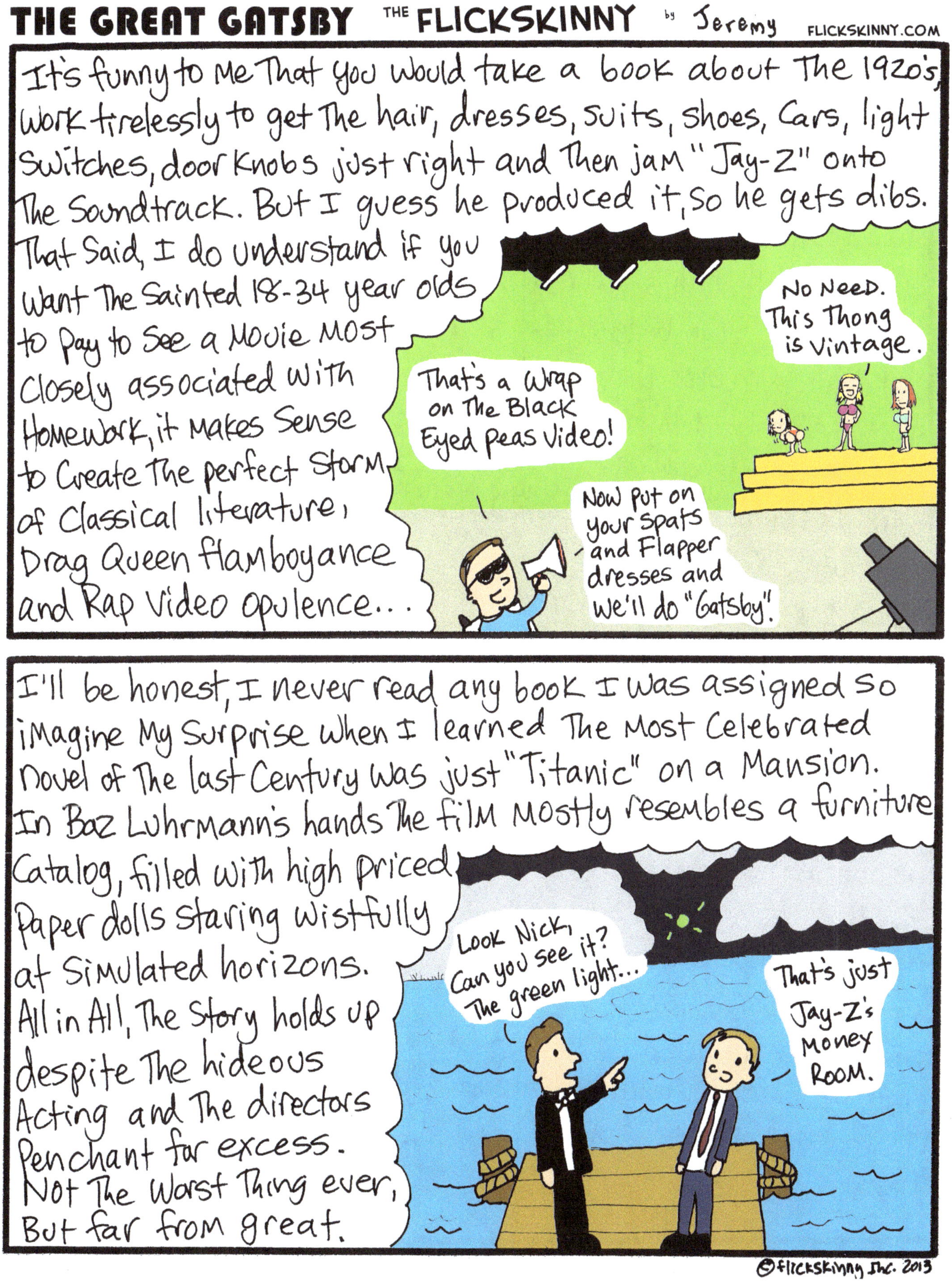
THE GREAT GATSBY
THE FLICKSKINNY by Jeremy
FLICKSKINNY.COM
It's funny to me that you would take a book about the 1920's, work tirelessly to get the hair, dresses, suits, shoes, cars, light switches, door knobs just right and then jam "Jay-Z" onto the soundtrack. But I guess he produced it, so he gets dibs.
That said, I do understand if you want the sainted 18-34 year olds to pay to see a movie most closely associated with homework, it makes sense to create the perfect storm of classical literature, drag queen flamboyance and rap video opulence...
No need. This thong is vintage.
That's a wrap on the Black Eyed Peas video!
Now put on your spats and flapper dresses and we'll do "Gatsby".
I'll be honest, I never read any book I was assigned so imagine my surprise when I learned the most celebrated novel of the last century was just "Titanic" on a mansion. In Baz Luhrmann's hands the film mostly resembles a furniture catalog, filled with high priced paper dolls staring wistfully at simulated horizons.
All in all, the story holds up despite the hideous acting and the directors penchant for excess. Not the worst thing ever, but far from great.
Look Nick, can you see it? The green light...
That's just Jay-Z's money room.
©flickskinny Inc. 2013

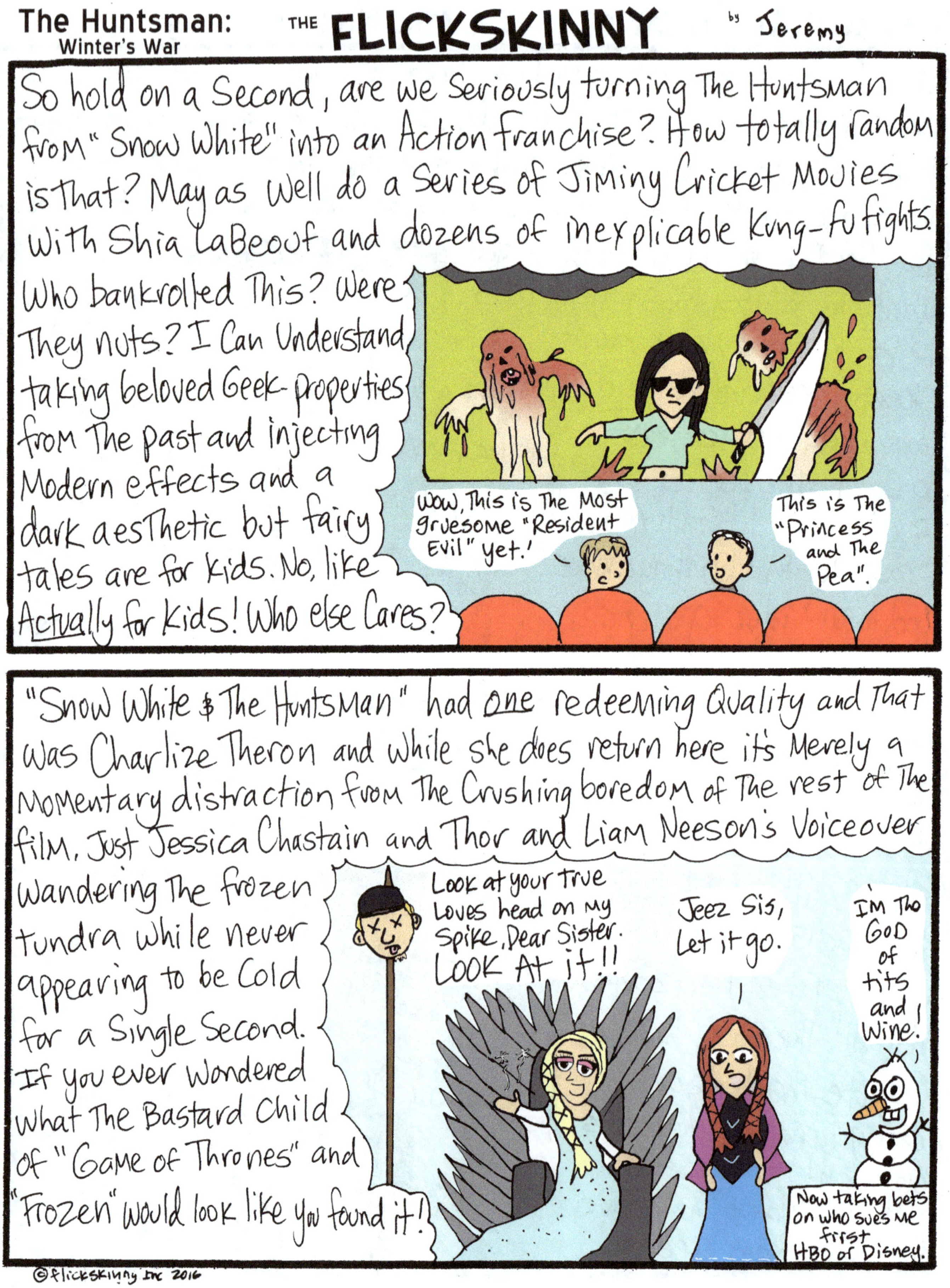
The Huntsman: Winter's War
THE FLICKSKINNY by Jeremy
So hold on a Second, are we Seriously turning The Huntsman from "Snow White" into an Action franchise? How totally random is That? May as well do a Series of Jiminy Cricket Movies with Shia LaBeouf and dozens of inexplicable Kung-fu fights.
Who bankrolled This? Were They nuts? I Can Understand taking beloved Geek-properties from The past and injecting Modern effects and a dark aesThetic but fairy tales are for kids. No, like Actually for Kids! Who else Cares?
Wow, This is The Most gruesome "Resident Evil" yet.
This is The "Princess and The Pea".
"Snow White & The Huntsman" had one redeeming Quality and That Was Charlize Theron and while she does return here it's Merely a Momentary distraction from The Crushing boredom of The rest of The film. Just Jessica Chastain and Thor and Liam Neeson's Voiceover
wandering The frozen tundra while never appearing to be Cold for a Single Second. If you ever wondered what The Bastard Child of "Game of Thrones" and "Frozen" would look like you found it!
Look at your True Loves head on My Spike, Dear Sister. LOOK AT it!!
Jeez Sis, Let it go.
I'M The GOD of tits and Wine!
Now taking bets on who sues Me first HBO or Disney.
©flickskinny Inc 2016

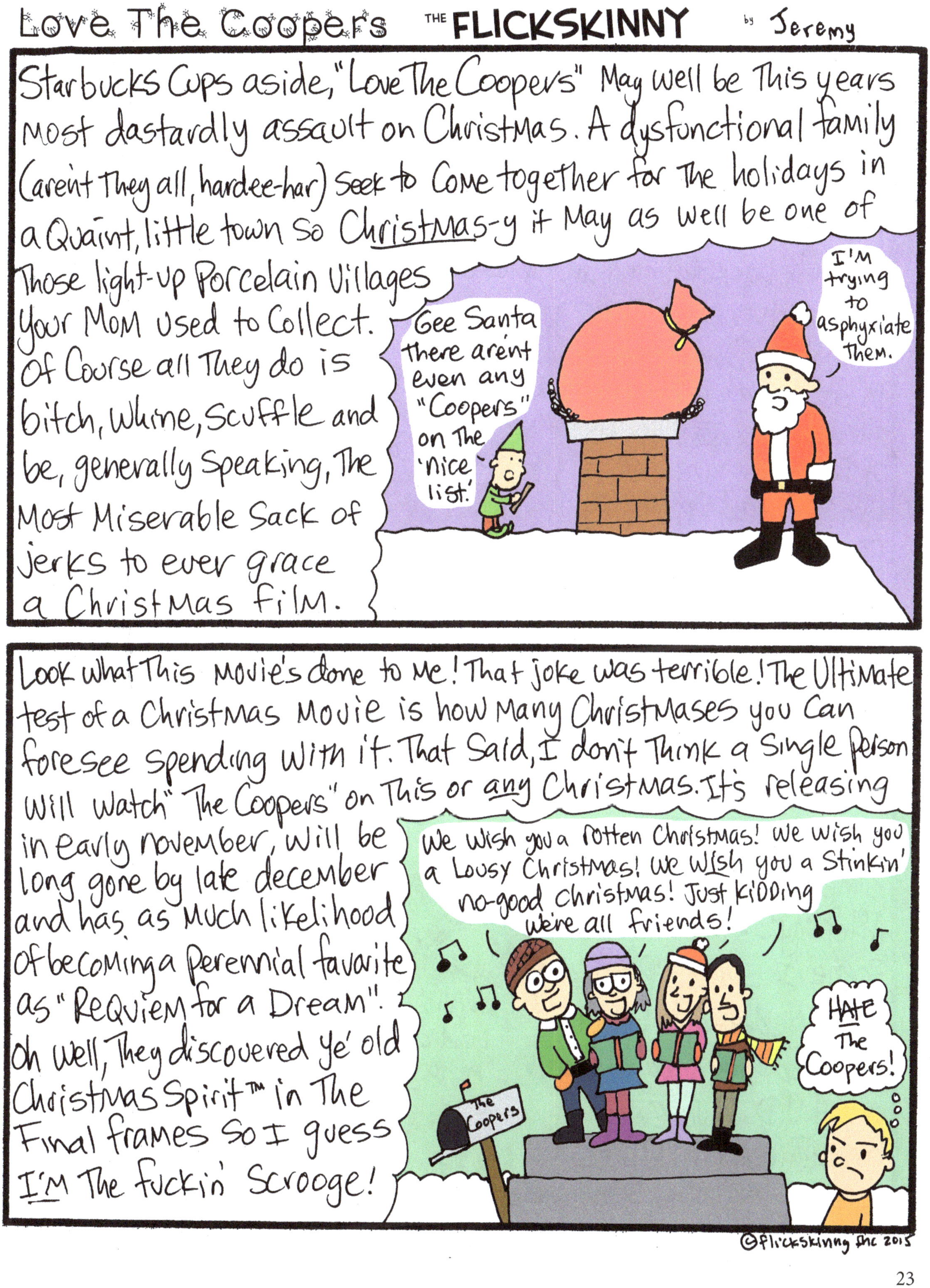
Love The Coopers
THE FLICKSKINNY by Jeremy
Starbucks Cups aside, "Love The Coopers" May well be This years Most dastardly assault on Christmas. A dysfunctional family (aren't They all, hardee-har) seek to Come together for The holidays in a Quaint, little town so Christmas-y it May as well be one of Those light-up Porcelain Villages your MoM used to Collect. Of Course all They do is bitch, whine, Scuffle and be, generally Speaking, The Most Miserable Sack of jerks to ever grace a Christmas film.
Gee Santa there aren't even any "Coopers" on The 'nice list.'
I'M trying to asphyxiate Them.
Look what This Movie's done to Me! That joke was terrible! The Ultimate test of a Christmas Movie is how Many Christmases you Can foresee spending with it. That Said, I don't Think a Single Person Will watch "The Coopers" on This or any Christmas. It's releasing in early november, will be long gone by late december and has as Much likelihood of becoming a Perennial favorite as "Requiem for a Dream". Oh well, They discovered ye' old Christmas Spirit™ in The Final frames So I guess I'M The fuckin' Scrooge!
We wish you a rotten Christmas! We wish you a Lousy Christmas! We wish you a Stinkin' no-good Christmas! Just kidding we're all friends!
HATE The Coopers!
The Coopers
©flickskinny inc 2015

SANCTUM a FLICKSKINNY by Jeremy

FLICKSKINNY.COM

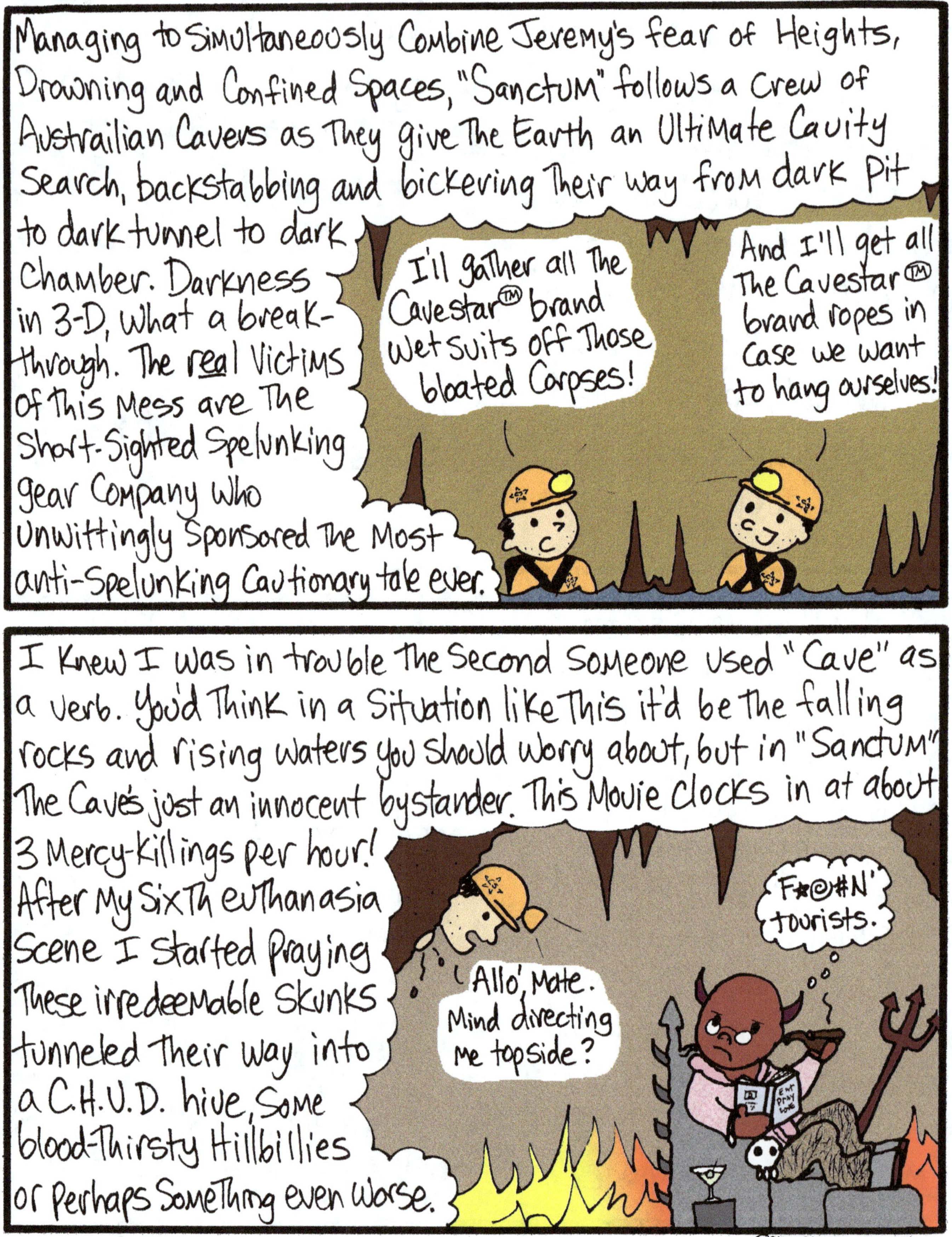
Managing to Simultaneoosly Combine Jeremy's fear of Heights, Drowning and Confined Spaces, "Sanctum" follows a Crew of Austrailian Cavers as They give The Earth an Ultimate Cavity Search, backstabbing and bickering Their way from dark Pit to dark tunnel to dark Chamber. Darkness in 3-D, What a break-through. The real Victims of This Mess are The Short-Sighted Spelunking gear Company who Unwittingly Sponsored The Most anti-Spelunking Cautionary tale ever.
I'll gather all The Cavestar™ brand Wet Suits off Those bloated Corpses!
And I'll get all The Cavestar™ brand ropes in case we want to hang ourselves!
I Knew I was in trouble The Second Someone Used "Cave" as a verb. You'd Think in a Situation like This it'd be The falling rocks and rising waters you Should worry about, but in "Sanctum" The Cave's just an innocent bystander. This Movie clocks in at about 3 Mercy-Killings per hour! After My SixTh euThanasia Scene I Started Praying These irredeeMable Skunks tunneled Their way into a C.H.U.D. hive, Some blood-Thirsty Hillbillies or Perhaps SomeThing even Worse.
Allo' Mate. Mind directing me topside?
F*@#N' tourists.

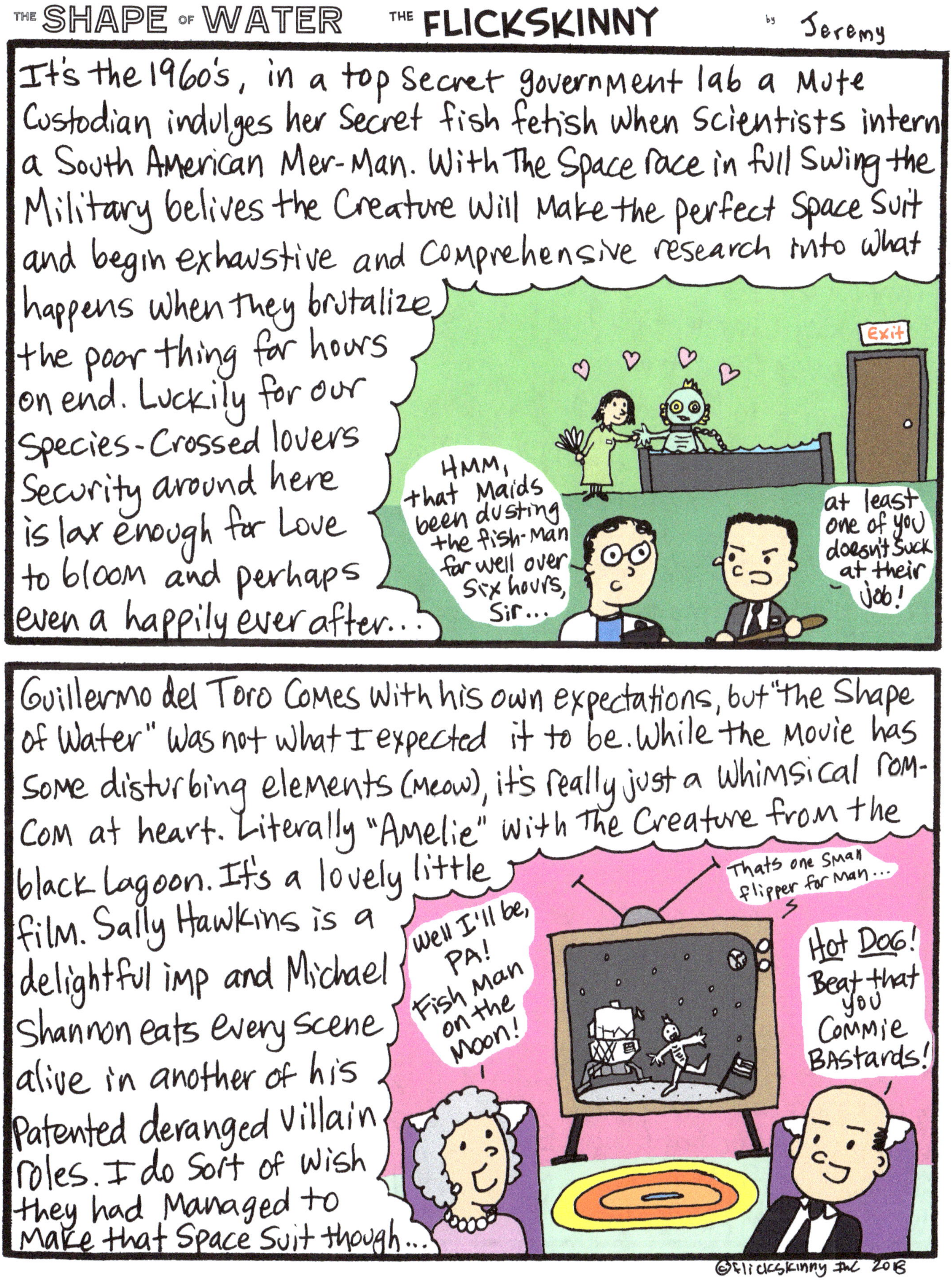
THE SHAPE OF WATER
THE FLICKSKINNY
by Jeremy
It's the 1960's, in a top secret government lab a mute custodian indulges her secret fish fetish when scientists intern a South American Mer-Man. With The Space race in full swing the Military belives the Creature will make the perfect space suit and begin exhaustive and comprehensive research into what happens when they brutalize the poor thing for hours on end. Luckily for our species-crossed lovers security around here is lax enough for love to bloom and perhaps even a happily ever after...
Exit
HMM, that Maids been dusting the fish-man for well over six hours, Sir...
at least one of you doesn't suck at their job!
Guillermo del Toro comes with his own expectations, but "the Shape of Water" was not what I expected it to be. While the movie has some disturbing elements (meow), it's really just a whimsical rom-com at heart. Literally "Amelie" with The Creature from the black Lagoon. It's a lovely little film. Sally Hawkins is a delightful imp and Michael Shannon eats every scene alive in another of his patented deranged villain roles. I do sort of wish they had managed to make that space suit though...
Thats one small flipper for man...
Well I'll be, PA! Fish man on the Moon!
Hot Dog! Beat that you commie Bastards!
©flickskinny inc 2018

THE
TREE OF LIFE
A **FLICKSKINNY** by Jeremy

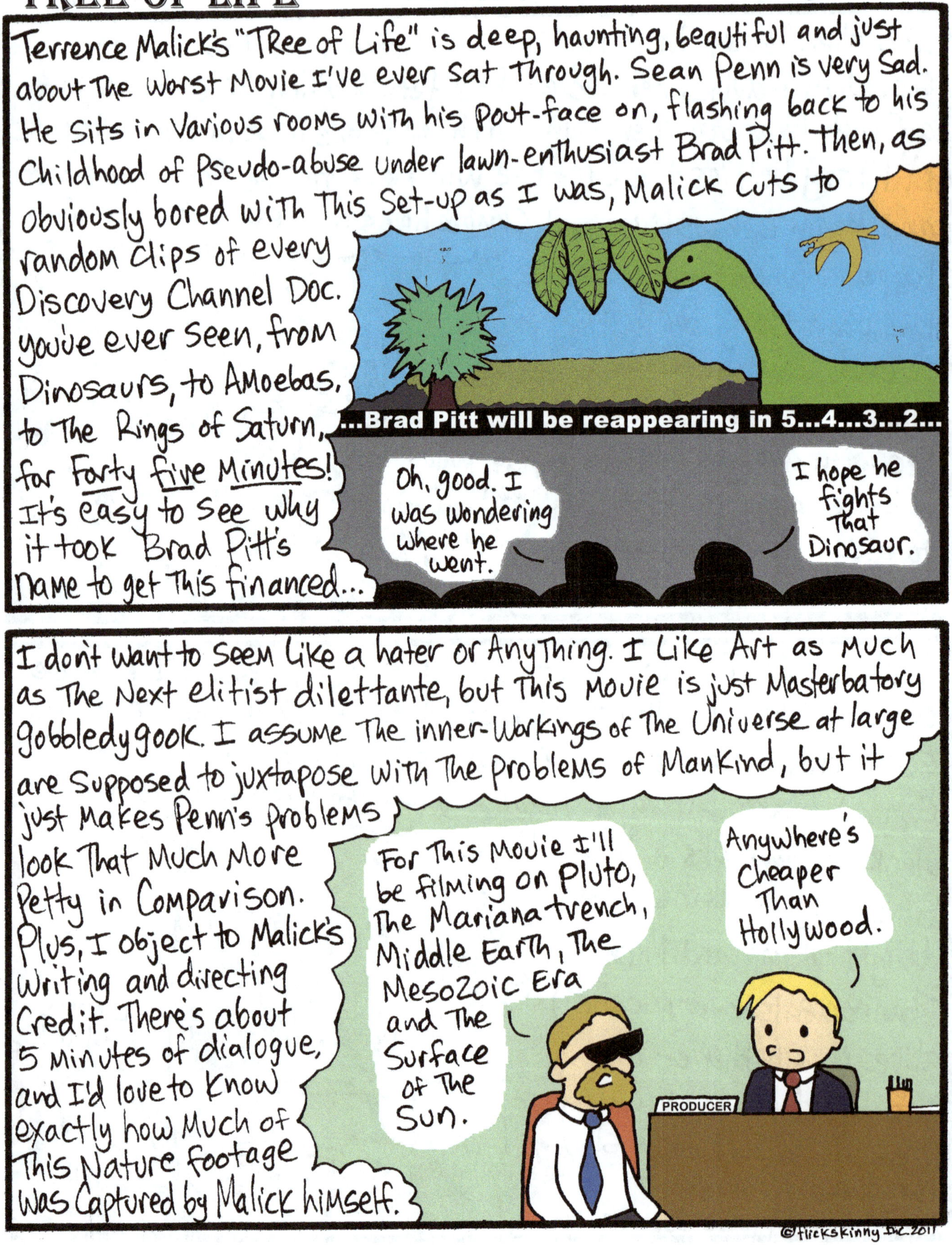

Terrence Malick's "Tree of Life" is deep, haunting, beautiful and just about The worst Movie I've ever sat Through. Sean Penn is very sad. He sits in Various rooms with his pout-face on, flashing back to his Childhood of pseudo-abuse under lawn-enthusiast Brad Pitt. Then, as obviously bored with This Set-up as I was, Malick Cuts to random Clips of every Discovery Channel Doc. you've ever Seen, from Dinosaurs, to Amoebas, to The Rings of Saturn, for Forty five Minutes! It's easy to see why it took Brad Pitt's name to get This financed...
...Brad Pitt will be reappearing in 5...4...3...2...
Oh, good. I was wondering where he went.
I hope he fights That Dinosaur.
I don't want to Seem like a hater or AnyThing. I Like Art as Much as The Next elitist dilettante, but This Movie is just Masterbatory gobbledygook. I assume The inner-Workings of The Universe at large are supposed to juxtapose with The problems of ManKind, but it just Makes Penn's problems look That Much More Petty in Comparison. Plus, I object to Malick's writing and directing Credit. There's about 5 Minutes of dialogue, and I'd love to Know exactly how Much of This Nature footage was Captured by Malick himself.
For This Movie I'll be filming on Pluto, The Mariana Trench, Middle Earth, The Mesozoic Era and The Surface of The Sun.
Anywhere's Cheaper Than Hollywood.
PRODUCER

Twilight: New Moon A **FLICKSKINNY** by Jeremy FLICKSKINNY.COM

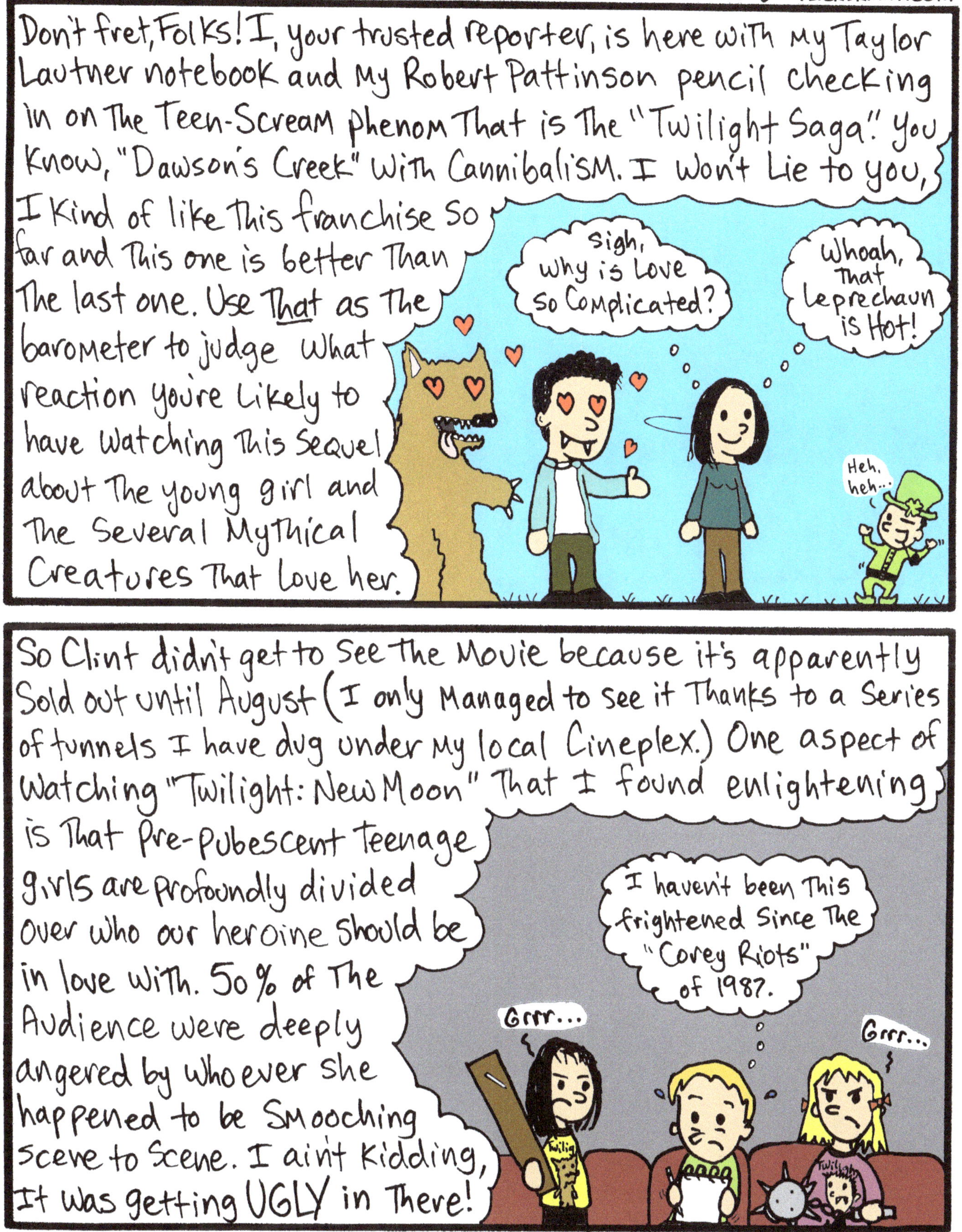
Don't fret, Folks! I, your trusted reporter, is here with my Taylor Lautner notebook and my Robert Pattinson pencil checking in on the Teen-Scream phenom that is the "Twilight Saga." You know, "Dawson's Creek" with Cannibalism. I won't lie to you, I kind of like this franchise so far and this one is better than the last one. Use that as the barometer to judge what reaction you're likely to have watching this sequel about the young girl and the several mythical creatures that love her.
Sigh, why is love so complicated?
Whoah, that leprechaun is hot!
Heh, heh...
So Clint didn't get to see the movie because it's apparently sold out until August (I only managed to see it thanks to a series of tunnels I have dug under my local Cineplex.) One aspect of watching "Twilight: New Moon" that I found enlightening is that pre-pubescent teenage girls are profoundly divided over who our heroine should be in love with. 50% of the audience were deeply angered by whoever she happened to be smooching scene to scene. I ain't kidding, it was getting UGLY in there!
I haven't been this frightened since the "Corey Riots" of 1987.
Grrr...
Grrr...
Twilig
Twilight

HORROR!

Finally her Soul and This franchise is at rest...
Psych! You have to burn The Japanese bones! I'M just The remake!

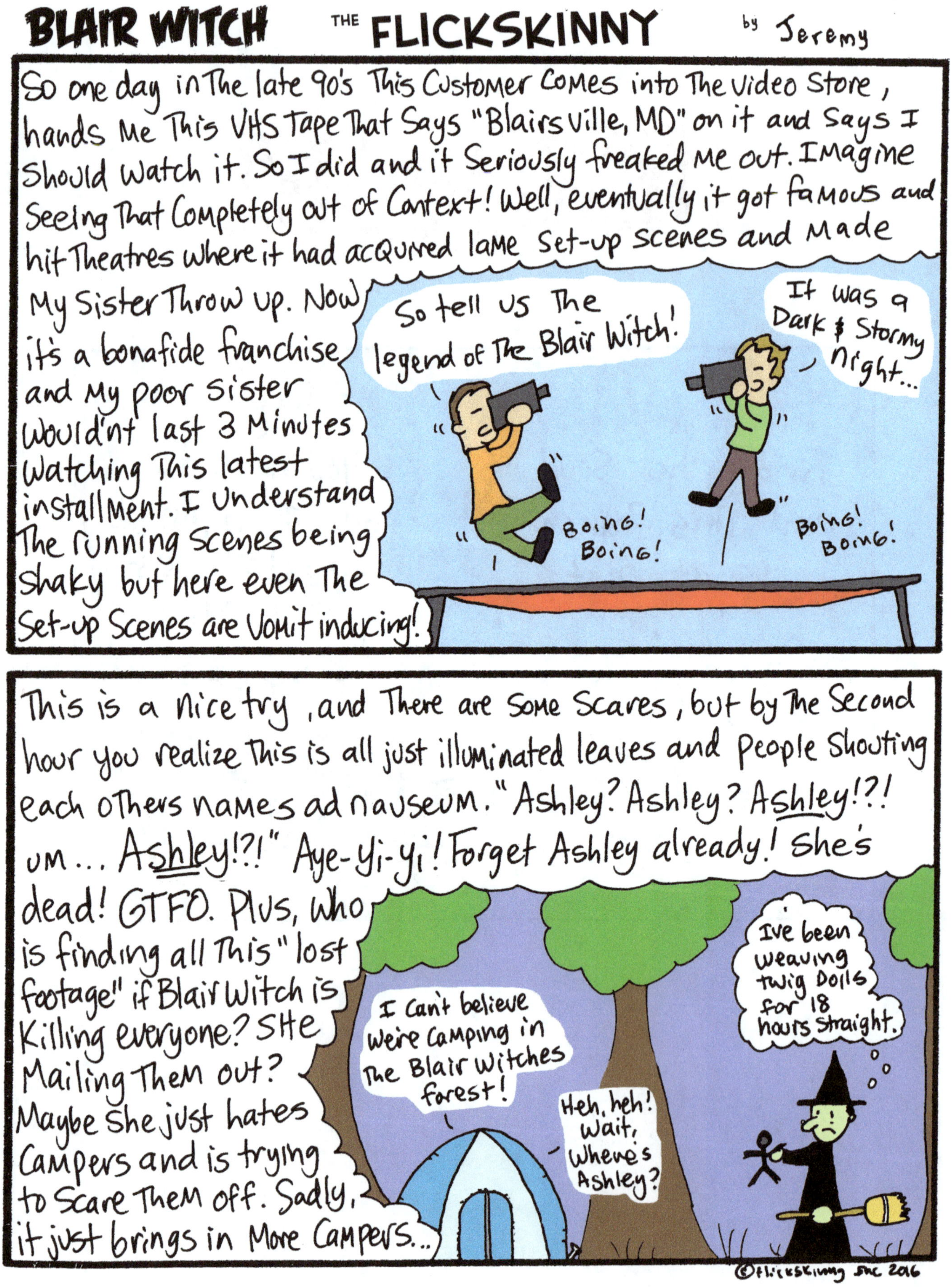
BLAIR WITCH
THE FLICKSKINNY by Jeremy
So one day in The late 90's This Customer Comes into The Video Store, hands Me This VHS Tape That Says "Blairsville, MD" on it and Says I Should watch it. So I did and it Seriously freaked Me out. Imagine Seeing That Completely out of Context! Well, eventually it got famous and hit Theatres where it had acquired lame Set-up scenes and Made My Sister Throw up. Now it's a bonafide franchise and My poor sister would'nt last 3 Minutes watching This latest installment. I Understand The running Scenes being shaky but here even The Set-up Scenes are Vomit inducing!
So tell us The legend of The Blair Witch!
It was a Dark & Stormy night...
Boing! Boing!
Boing! Boing!
This is a nice try, and There are Some Scares, but by The Second hour you realize This is all just illuminated leaves and people Shouting each Others names ad nauseum. "Ashley? Ashley? Ashley!?! um... Ashley!?!" Aye-yi-yi! Forget Ashley already! She's dead! GTFO. Plus, who is finding all This "lost footage" if Blair Witch is Killing everyone? SHe Mailing Them out? Maybe She just hates Campers and is trying to Scare Them off. Sadly, it just brings in More Campers...
I Can't believe we're Camping in The Blair Witches forest!
Heh, heh! Wait, Where's Ashley?
I've been weaving twig Dolls for 18 hours Straight.
©FlickSkinny Inc 2016

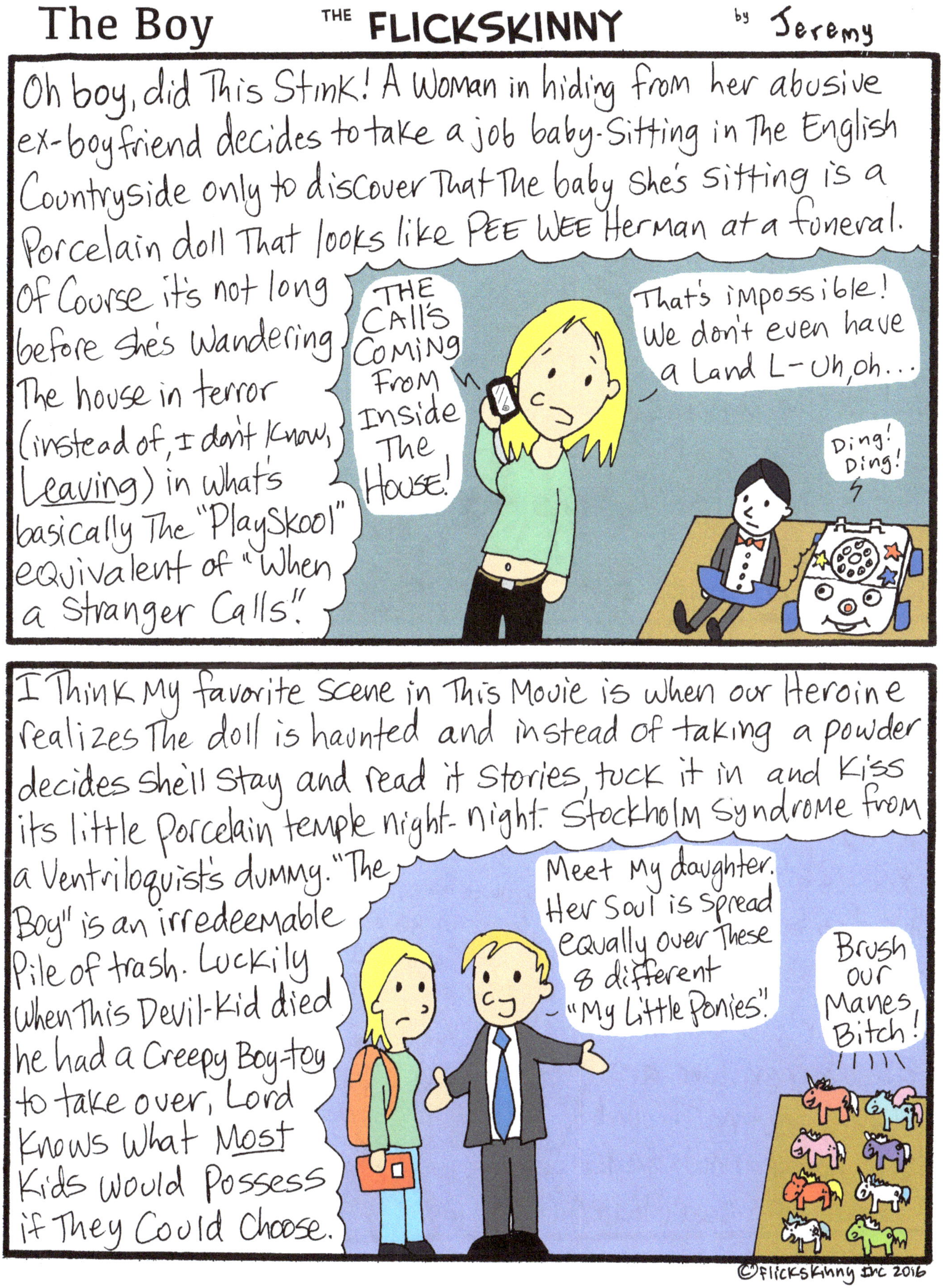
The Boy
THE FLICKSKINNY
by Jeremy
Oh boy, did This Stink! A Woman in hiding from her abusive ex-boyfriend decides to take a job baby-Sitting in The English Countryside only to discover That The baby She's Sitting is a Porcelain doll That looks like PEE WEE Herman at a funeral.
Of Course it's not long before she's Wandering The house in terror (instead of, I don't Know, Leaving) in what's basically The "PlaySkool" equivalent of "When a Stranger Calls".
THE CALL'S COMING FROM Inside The House!
That's impossible! We don't even have a Land L-Uh, oh...
Ding! Ding!
I Think My favorite Scene in This Movie is when our Heroine realizes The doll is haunted and instead of taking a powder decides She'll Stay and read it Stories, tuck it in and Kiss its little Porcelain temple night-night. Stockholm Syndrome from a Ventriloquist's dummy. "The Boy" is an irredeemable Pile of trash. Luckily when This Devil-Kid died he had a Creepy Boy-toy to take over, Lord Knows What Most Kids would Possess if They Could Choose.
Meet My daughter. Her Soul is Spread equally over These 8 different "My Little Ponies".
Brush our Manes Bitch!
©FlickSkinny Inc 2016

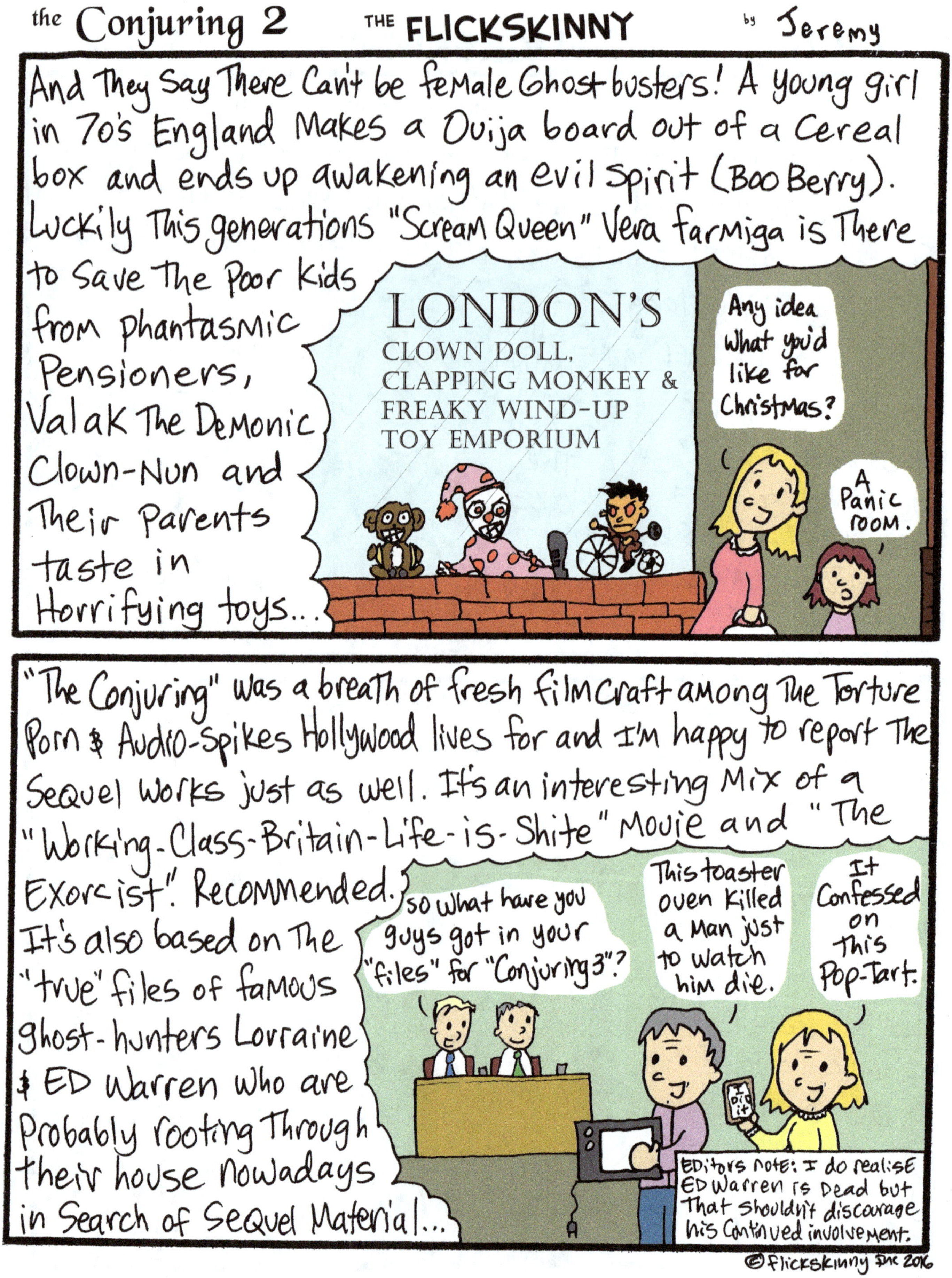
the Conjuring 2
THE FLICKSKINNY
by Jeremy
And They Say There Can't be feMale Ghost busters! A young girl in 70's England Makes a Ouija board out of a Cereal box and ends up awakening an evil Spirit (Boo Berry). Luckily This generations "Scream Queen" Vera farMiga is There to Save The Poor Kids from phantasMic Pensioners, Valak The DeMonic Clown-Nun and Their Parents taste in Horrifying toys...
LONDON'S
CLOWN DOLL, CLAPPING MONKEY & FREAKY WIND-UP TOY EMPORIUM
Any idea what you'd like for Christmas?
A Panic room.
"The Conjuring" was a breath of fresh filmCraft among The Torture Porn & Audio-Spikes Hollywood lives for and I'M happy to report The Sequel works just as well. It's an interesting Mix of a "Working-Class-Britain-Life-is-Shite" Movie and "The Exorcist". ReCommended. It's also based on The "true" files of famous ghost-hunters Lorraine & ED Warren who are Probably rooting Through their house nowadays in Search of SeQuel Material...
so what have you guys got in your "files" for "Conjuring 3"?
This toaster oven Killed a Man just to watch him die.
It Confessed on This Pop-Tart.
I Did It
EDitors note: I do realise ED Warren is Dead but That shouldn't discourage his Continued involvement.
©flickskinny Inc 2016

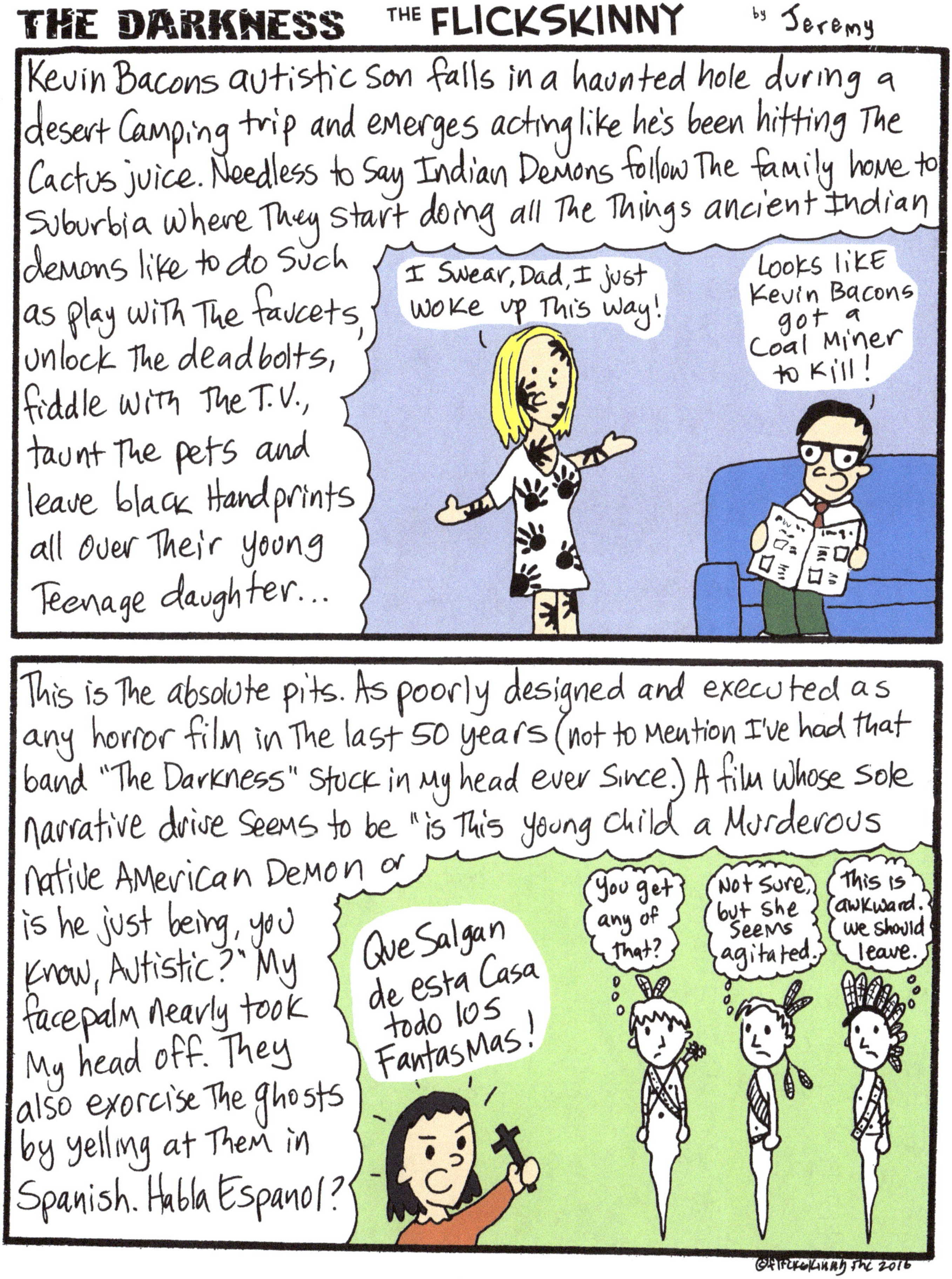
THE DARKNESS
THE FLICKSKINNY
by Jeremy
Kevin Bacons autistic son falls in a haunted hole during a desert Camping trip and emerges acting like he's been hitting The Cactus juice. Needless to Say Indian Demons follow The family home to Suburbia where They start doing all The Things ancient Indian demons like to do Such as play with The faucets, unlock The deadbolts, fiddle with The T.V., taunt The pets and leave black Handprints all over Their young Teenage daughter...
I Swear, Dad, I just woke up This way!
Looks like Kevin Bacons got a Coal Miner to Kill!
This is The absolute pits. As poorly designed and executed as any horror film in The last 50 years (not to Mention I've had that band "The Darkness" stuck in My head ever Since.) A film whose sole narrative drive Seems to be "is This young Child a Murderous native American Demon or is he just being, you know, Autistic?" My facepalm nearly took My head off. They also exorcise The ghosts by yelling at Them in Spanish. Habla Espanol?
Que Salgan de esta Casa todo los FantasMas!
You get any of That?
Not Sure, but She Seems agitated.
This is awkward. we should leave.
2016

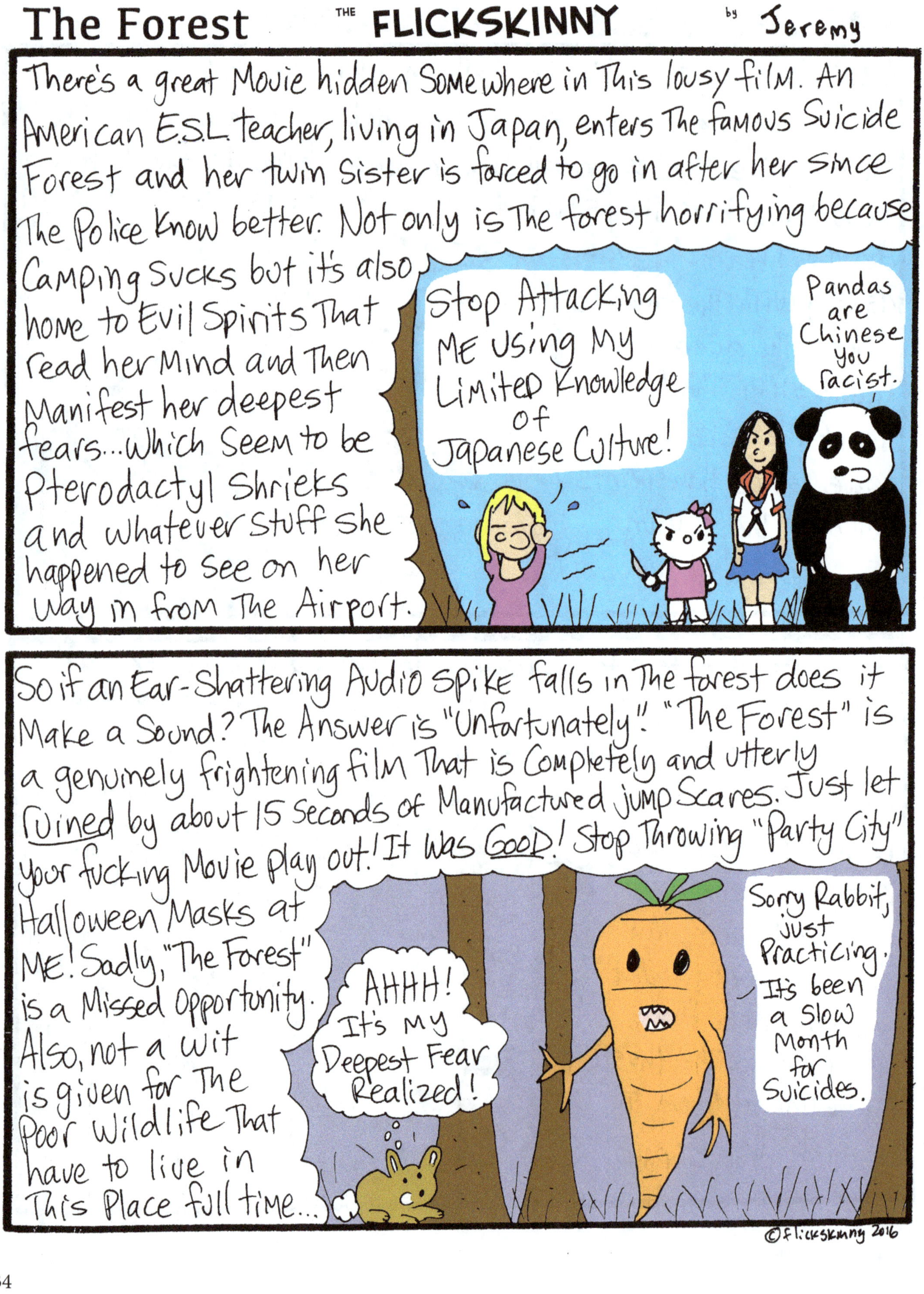
The Forest
THE FLICKSKINNY
by Jeremy
There's a great Movie hidden Somewhere in This lousy film. An American E.S.L. teacher, living in Japan, enters The famous Suicide Forest and her twin Sister is forced to go in after her since The Police Know better. Not only is The forest horrifying because Camping Sucks but it's also home to Evil Spirits That read her Mind and Then Manifest her deepest fears...Which Seem to be Pterodactyl Shrieks and whatever Stuff She happened to See on her way in from The Airport.
Stop Attacking ME using My Limited Knowledge of Japanese Culture!
Pandas are Chinese you racist.
So if an Ear-Shattering Audio Spike falls in The forest does it Make a Sound? The Answer is "Unfortunately." "The Forest" is a genuinely frightening film That is Completely and utterly Ruined by about 15 Seconds of Manufactured jump Scares. Just let your fucking Movie play out! It was GOOD! Stop Throwing "Party City" Halloween Masks at ME! Sadly, "The Forest" is a Missed Opportunity. Also, not a wit is given for The Poor Wildlife That have to live in This Place full time...
AHHH! It's My Deepest Fear Realized!
Sorry Rabbit, just Practicing. It's been a Slow Month for Suicides.
©flickskinny 2016

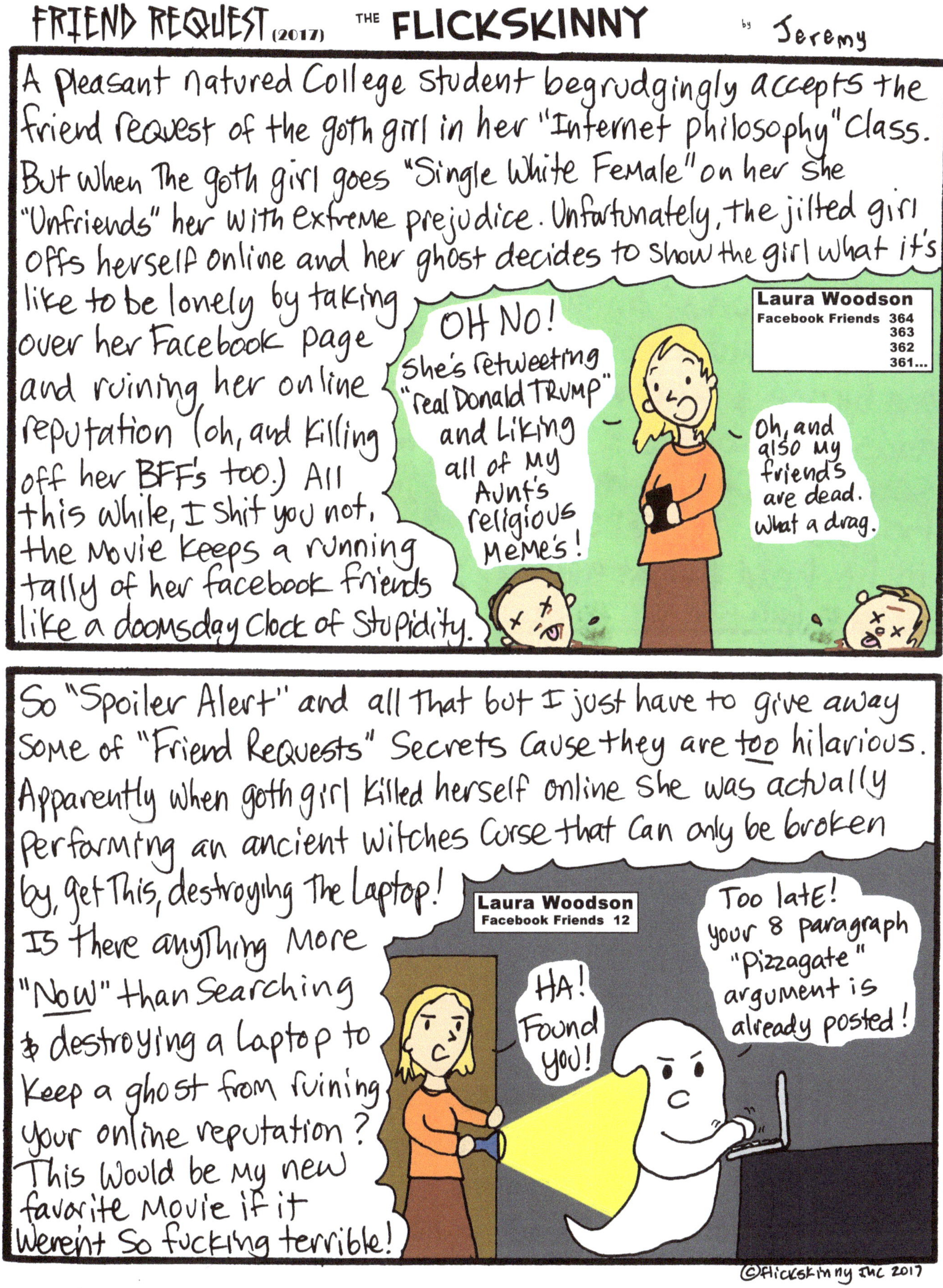
FRIEND REQUEST (2017)
THE FLICKSKINNY
by Jeremy
A pleasant natured College student begrudgingly accepts the friend request of the goth girl in her "Internet philosophy" Class. But when The goth girl goes "Single White Female" on her she "Unfriends" her with extreme prejudice. Unfortunately, the jilted girl offs herself online and her ghost decides to show the girl what it's like to be lonely by taking over her Facebook page and ruining her online reputation (oh, and killing off her BFF's too.) All this while, I shit you not, the Movie keeps a running tally of her facebook friends like a doomsday Clock of Stupidity.
Laura Woodson
Facebook Friends 364 363 362 361...
OH NO! She's retweeting "real Donald TRUMP" and Liking all of My Aunt's religious MeMe's!
Oh, and also my friend's are dead. What a drag.
So "Spoiler Alert" and all That but I just have to give away Some of "Friend Requests" Secrets Cause they are too hilarious. Apparently when goth girl Killed herself online She was actually performing an ancient witches Curse that Can only be broken by, get This, destroying The Laptop! IS there anything More "Now" than Searching & destroying a Laptop to Keep a ghost from ruining your online reputation? This Would be My new favorite Movie if it Weren't So fucking terrible!
Laura Woodson
Facebook Friends 12
HA! Found you!
Too latE! your 8 paragraph "Pizzagate" argument is already posted!
©Flickskinny Inc 2017

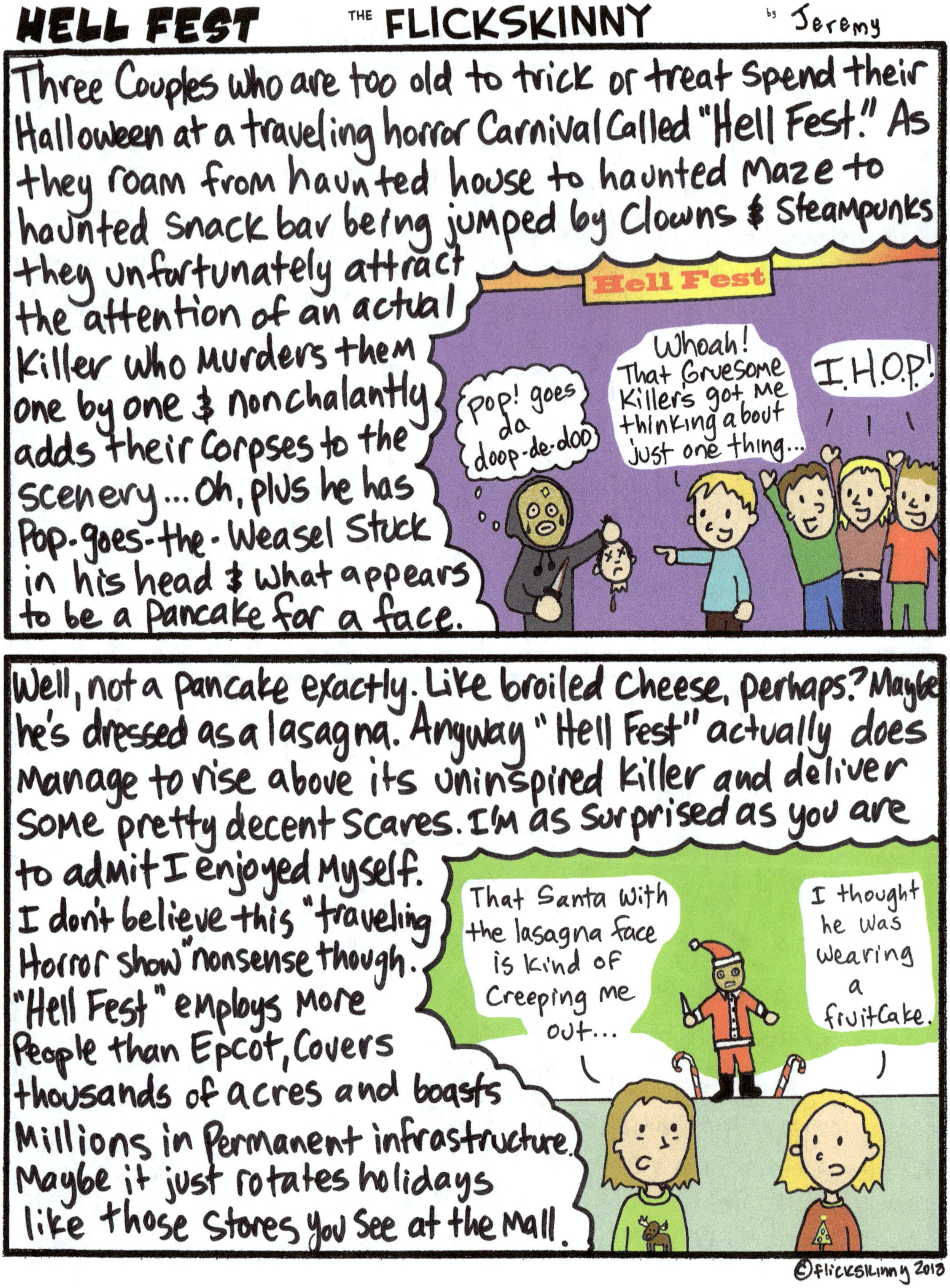
HELL FEST
THE FLICKSKINNY
by Jeremy
Three Couples who are too old to trick or treat Spend their Halloween at a traveling horror Carnival Called "Hell Fest." As they roam from haunted house to haunted Maze to haunted snack bar being jumped by Clowns & Steampunks they unfortunately attract the attention of an actual Killer who Murders them one by one & nonchalantly adds their Corpses to the scenery... Oh, plus he has Pop-goes-the-Weasel Stuck in his head & what appears to be a Pancake for a face.
Hell Fest
Pop! goes da doop-de-doo
Whoah! That Gruesome Killers got Me thinking about just one thing...
I.H.O.P!
Well, not a pancake exactly. Like broiled Cheese, perhaps? Maybe he's dressed as a lasagna. Anyway "Hell Fest" actually does Manage to rise above its uninspired Killer and deliver Some pretty decent Scares. I'm as surprised as you are to admit I enjoyed Myself. I don't believe this "traveling Horror show" nonsense though. "Hell Fest" employs More People than Epcot, Covers thousands of acres and boasts Millions in Permanent infrastructure. Maybe it just rotates holidays like those stores you See at the Mall.
That Santa with the lasagna face is kind of Creeping me out...
I thought he was wearing a fruitcake.
©flickskinny 2018

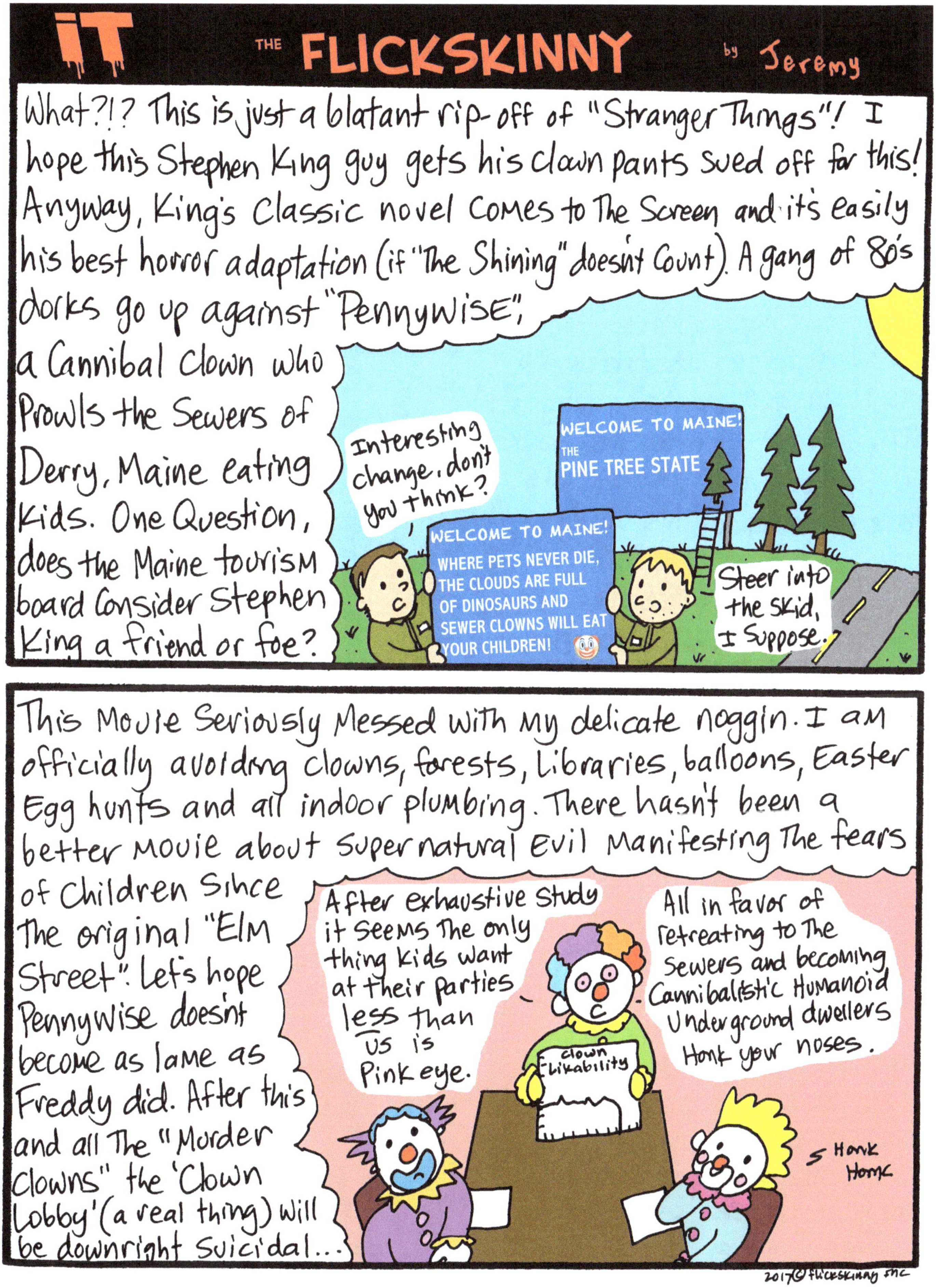
IT
THE FLICKSKINNY
by Jeremy
What?!? This is just a blatant rip-off of "Stranger Things"! I hope this Stephen King guy gets his clown pants sued off for this! Anyway, King's classic novel comes to the screen and it's easily his best horror adaptation (if "The Shining" doesn't count). A gang of 80's dorks go up against "Pennywise", a cannibal clown who prowls the sewers of Derry, Maine eating kids. One question, does the Maine tourism board consider Stephen King a friend or foe?
Interesting change, don't you think?
WELCOME TO MAINE! THE PINE TREE STATE
WELCOME TO MAINE! WHERE PETS NEVER DIE, THE CLOUDS ARE FULL OF DINOSAURS AND SEWER CLOWNS WILL EAT YOUR CHILDREN!
Steer into the skid, I suppose.
This movie seriously messed with my delicate noggin. I am officially avoiding clowns, forests, libraries, balloons, Easter Egg hunts and all indoor plumbing. There hasn't been a better movie about supernatural evil manifesting the fears of children since the original "Elm Street". Let's hope Pennywise doesn't become as lame as Freddy did. After this and all the "Murder Clowns" the 'Clown Lobby' (a real thing) will be downright suicidal...
After exhaustive study it seems the only thing kids want at their parties less than us is pink eye.
Clown Likability
All in favor of retreating to the sewers and becoming cannibalistic humanoid underground dwellers honk your noses.
Honk Honk
2017© flickskinny inc

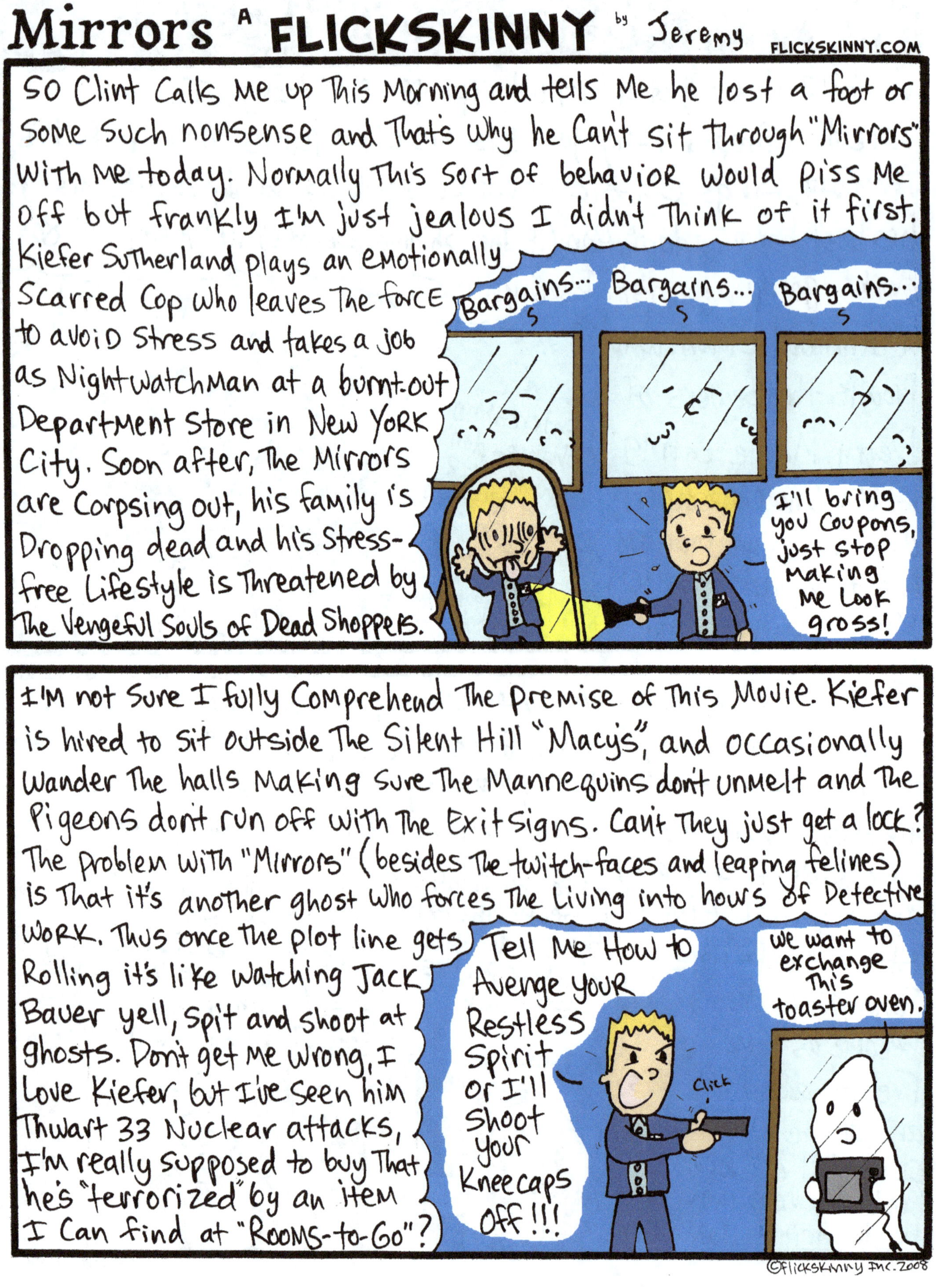
Mirrors A FLICKSKINNY by Jeremy
FLICKSKINNY.COM
So Clint Calls Me up This Morning and tells Me he lost a foot or Some Such nonsense and That's why he Can't sit through "Mirrors" With Me today. Normally This sort of behavior would piss Me off but frankly I'm just jealous I didn't Think of it first.
Kiefer Sutherland plays an emotionally Scarred Cop who leaves The force to avoid Stress and takes a job as Nightwatchman at a burnt-out Department Store in New York City. Soon after, The Mirrors are Corpsing out, his family is Dropping dead and his Stress-free Lifestyle is Threatened by The Vengeful Souls of Dead Shoppers.
Bargains...
Bargains...
Bargains...
I'll bring you Coupons, just stop making me look gross!
I'm not Sure I fully Comprehend The premise of This Movie. Kiefer is hired to sit outside The Silent Hill "Macy's" and occasionally Wander The halls Making sure The Mannequins don't unmelt and The Pigeons don't run off with The Exit Signs. Can't They just get a lock? The problem with "Mirrors" (besides The twitch-faces and leaping felines) is That it's another ghost who forces The Living into hours of Detective Work. Thus once the plot line gets Rolling it's like watching Jack Bauer yell, spit and shoot at ghosts. Don't get me wrong, I Love Kiefer, but I've seen him Thwart 33 Nuclear attacks, I'm really supposed to buy That he's "terrorized" by an item I Can find at "Rooms-to-Go"?
Tell Me How to Avenge your Restless Spirit or I'll Shoot your Kneecaps off!!!
Click
we want to exchange This toaster oven.
©Flickskinny Inc. 2008

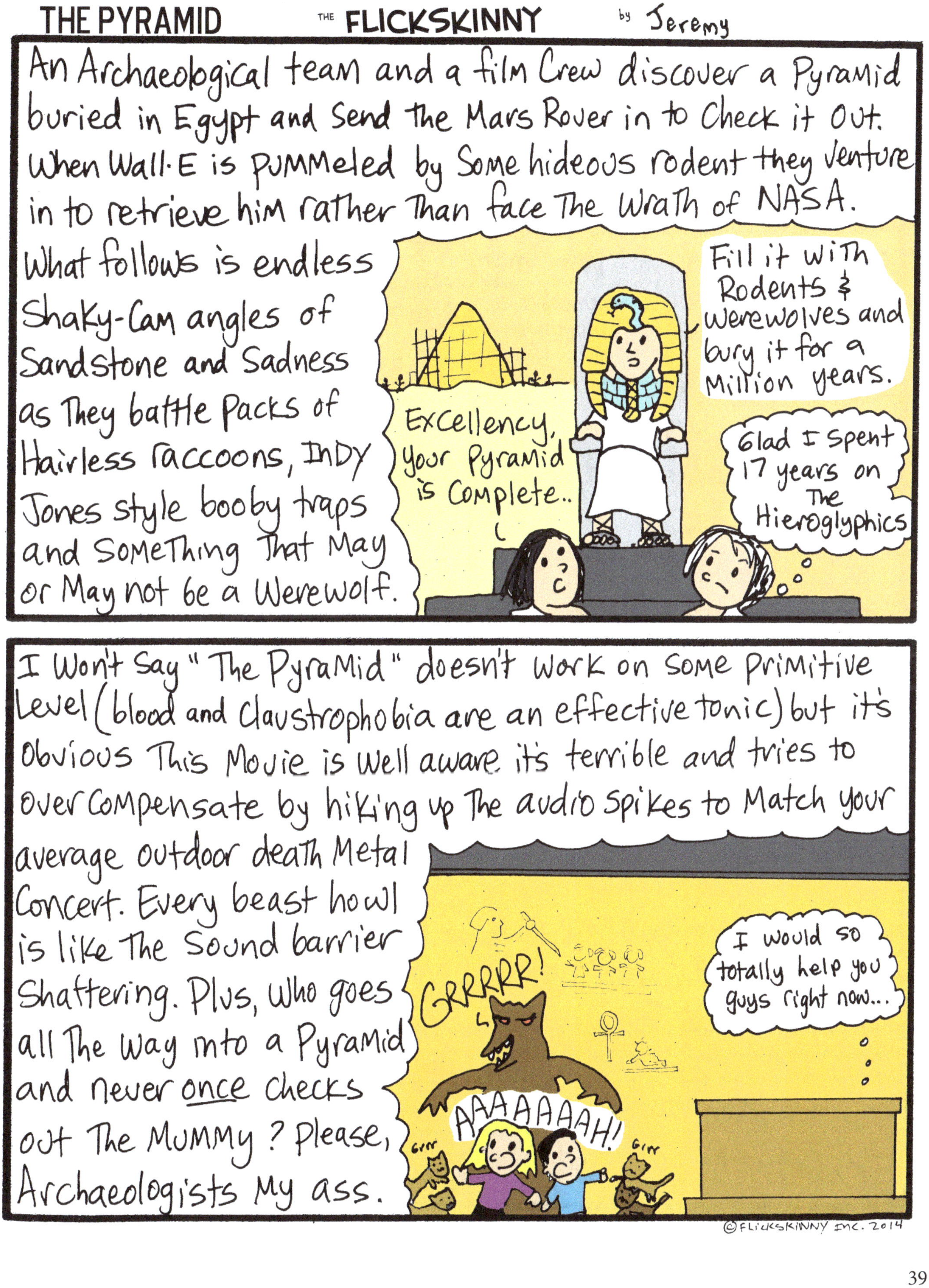
THE PYRAMID
THE FLICKSKINNY
by Jeremy
An Archaeological team and a film Crew discover a Pyramid buried in Egypt and Send the Mars Rover in to Check it Out. When Wall·E is pummeled by Some hideous rodent they venture in to retrieve him rather Than face The Wrath of NASA.
What follows is endless Shaky-Cam angles of Sandstone and Sadness as They battle Packs of Hairless raccoons, Indy Jones style booby traps and Something That May or May not be a Werewolf.
Excellency, your Pyramid is Complete..
Fill it with Rodents & werewolves and bury it for a Million years.
Glad I Spent 17 years on The Hieroglyphics
I Won't Say "The Pyramid" doesn't work on Some primitive Level (blood and Claustrophobia are an effective tonic) but it's obvious This Movie is Well aware it's terrible and tries to over compensate by hiking up The audio Spikes to Match your average outdoor death Metal Concert. Every beast howl is like The Sound barrier Shattering. Plus, who goes all The way into a Pyramid and never once checks out The Mummy? Please, Archaeologists My ass.
GRRRRR!
I would so totally help you guys right now...
AAAAAAAH!
Grrr
Grrr

The Thing

FLICKSKINNY by Jeremy

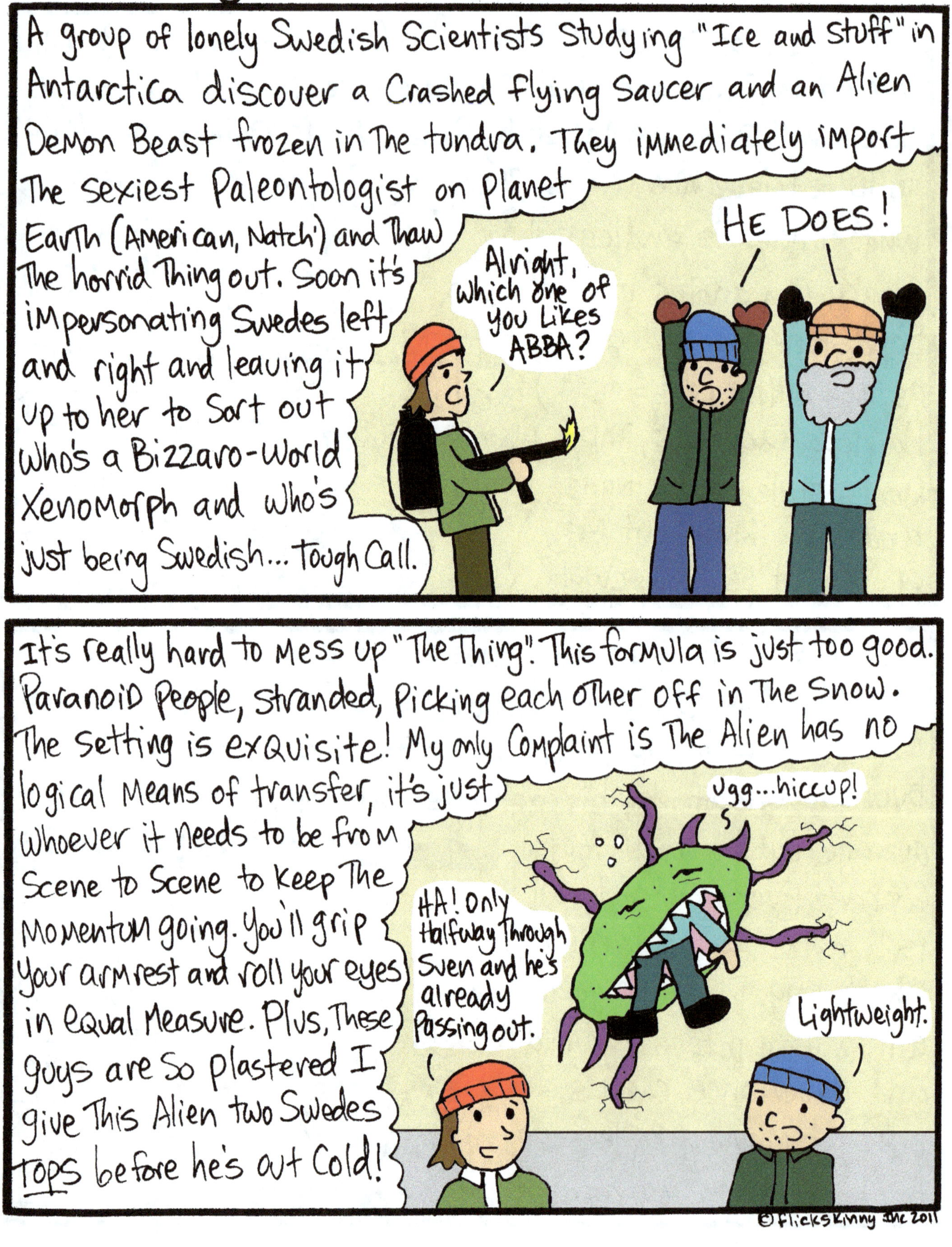

A group of lonely Swedish Scientists Studying "Ice and Stuff" in Antarctica discover a Crashed flying Saucer and an Alien Demon Beast frozen in The tundra. They immediately import The sexiest Paleontologist on Planet Earth (American, Natch) and Thaw The horrid Thing out. Soon it's impersonating Swedes left and right and leaving it up to her to Sort out who's a Bizzaro-World Xenomorph and who's just being Swedish... Tough Call.
Alright, which one of you Likes ABBA?
HE DOES!
It's really hard to Mess up "The Thing". This formula is just too good. Paranoid People, stranded, Picking each other off in The Snow. The Setting is exquisite! My only Complaint is The Alien has no logical Means of transfer, it's just whoever it needs to be from Scene to Scene to keep The Momentum going. You'll grip your armrest and roll your eyes in Equal Measure. Plus, These guys are So plastered I give This Alien two Swedes TOPS before he's out Cold!
Ugg...hiccup!
HA! Only Halfway Through Sven and he's already Passing out.
Lightweight.
©FlickSkinny Inc 2011

Music!

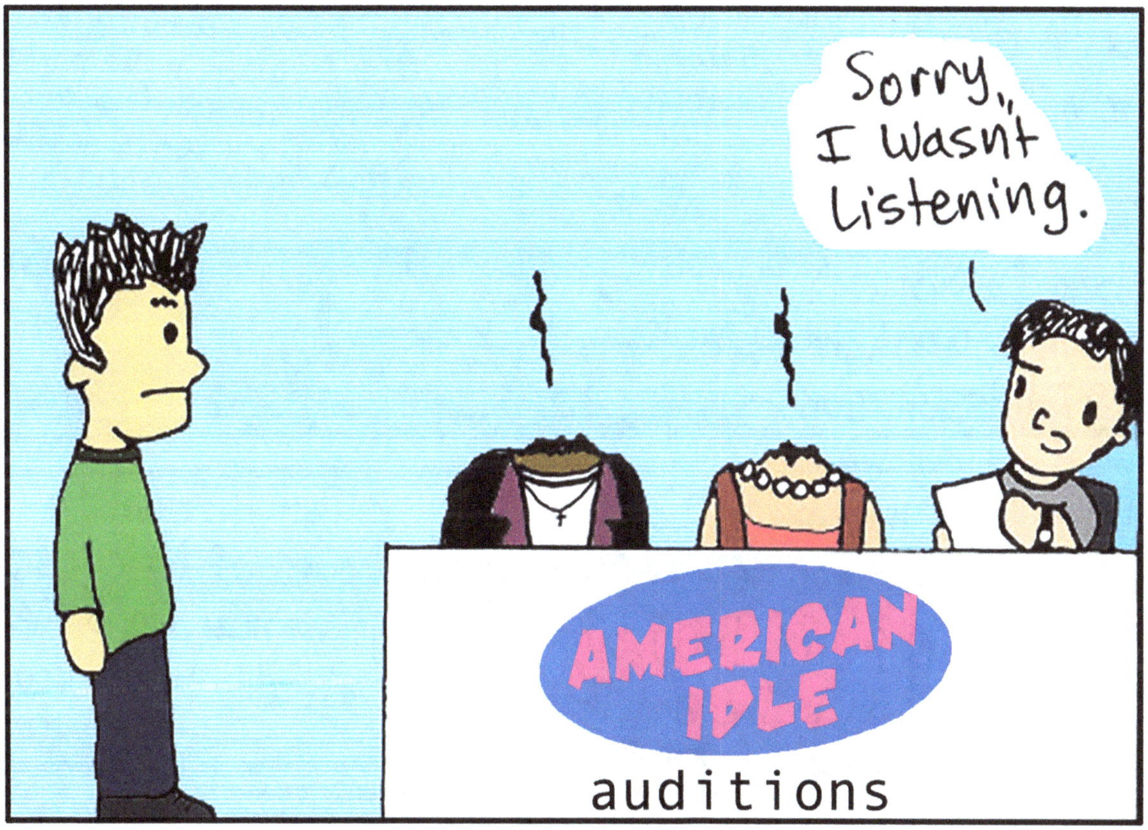
Sorry, I wasn't listening.
AMERICAN IDLE
auditions

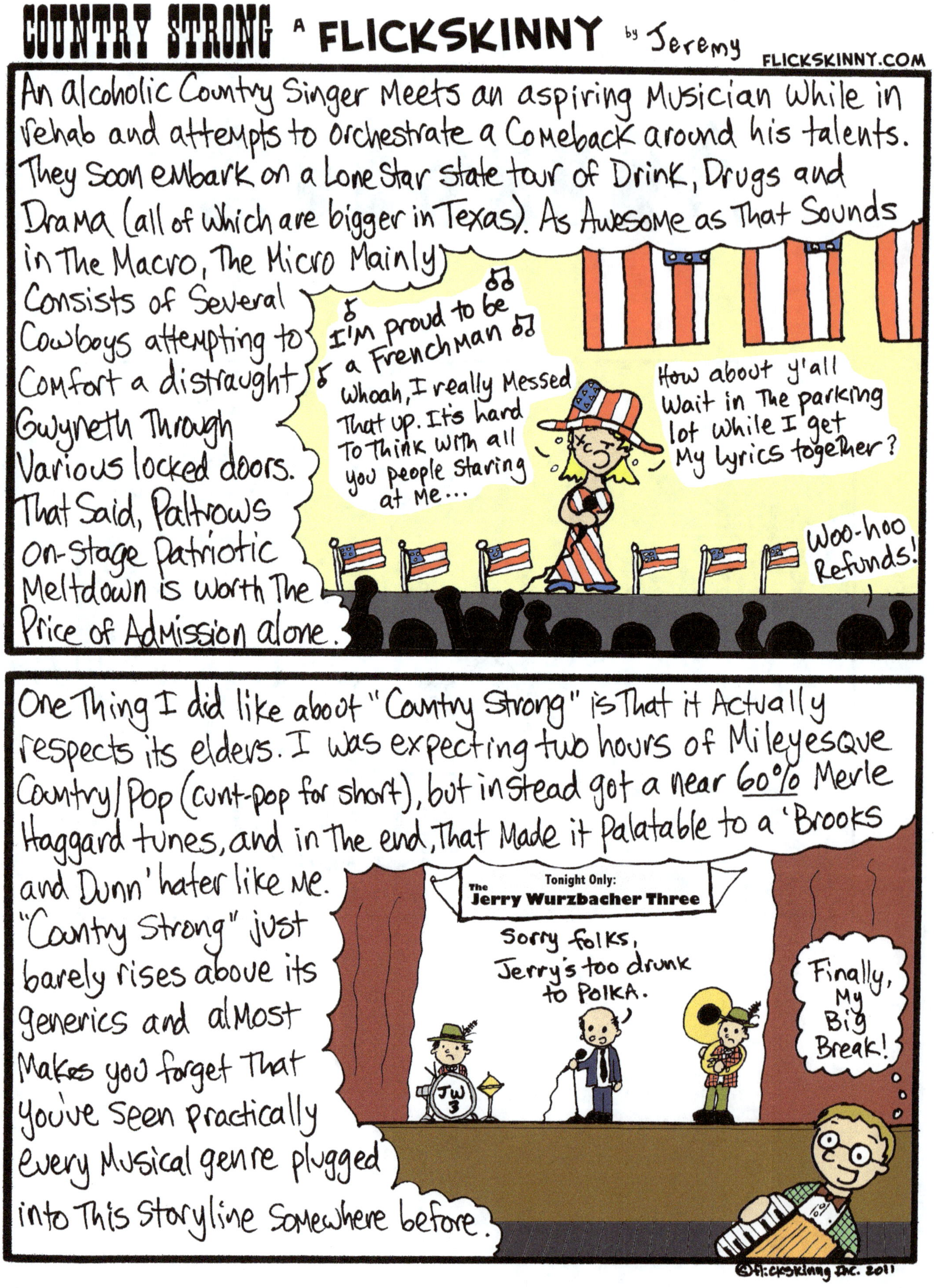
COUNTRY STRONG a FLICKSKINNY by Jeremy
FLICKSKINNY.COM
An alcoholic Country Singer Meets an aspiring Musician While in rehab and attempts to orchestrate a Comeback around his talents. They soon embark on a Lone Star State tour of Drink, Drugs and Drama (all of which are bigger in Texas). As Awesome as That Sounds in The Macro, The Micro Mainly Consists of Several Cowboys attempting to Comfort a distraught Gwyneth Through Various locked doors. That Said, Paltrows on-stage Patriotic Meltdown is worth The Price of Admission alone.
I'M proud to be a Frenchman
Whoah, I really Messed That up. It's hard To Think with all you people staring at Me...
How about y'all Wait in The parking lot while I get My lyrics together?
Woo-hoo Refunds!
One Thing I did like about "Country Strong" is That it Actually respects its elders. I was expecting two hours of Mileyesque Country/Pop (cunt-pop for short), but instead got a near 60% Merle Haggard tunes, and in The end, That Made it Palatable to a 'Brooks and Dunn' hater like me. "Country Strong" just barely rises above its generics and almost Makes you forget That you've seen practically every Musical genre plugged into This Storyline Somewhere before.
Tonight Only:
The Jerry Wurzbacher Three
Sorry folks, Jerry's too drunk to POLKA.
JW 3
Finally, My Big Break!
©Flickskinny Inc. 2011

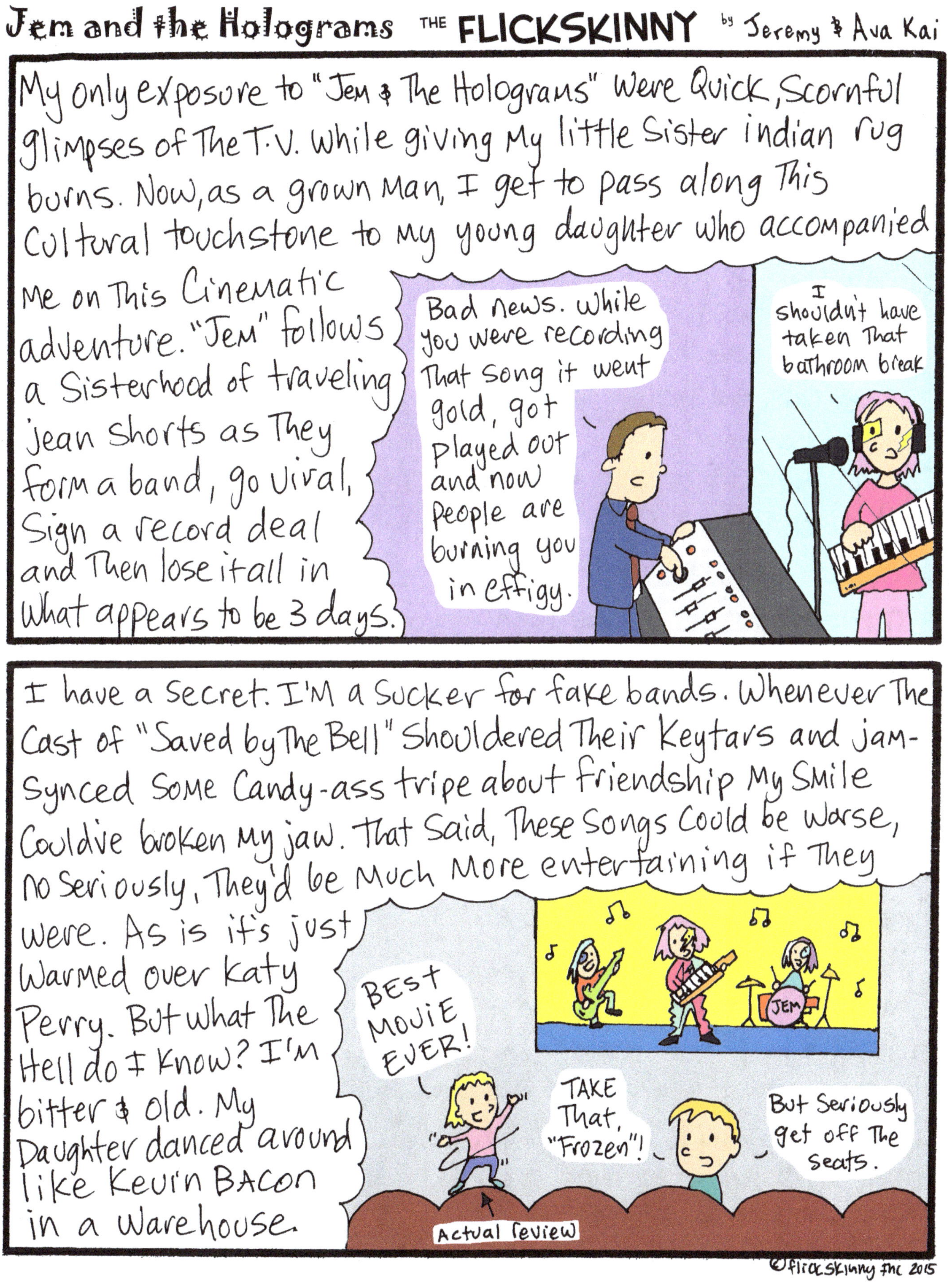
Jem and the Holograms
THE FLICKSKINNY
by Jeremy & Ava Kai
My only exposure to "Jem & The Holograms" were quick, scornful glimpses of The T.V. while giving my little sister indian rug burns. Now, as a grown man, I get to pass along this cultural touchstone to my young daughter who accompanied me on this cinematic adventure. "Jem" follows a sisterhood of traveling jean shorts as they form a band, go viral, sign a record deal and then lose it all in what appears to be 3 days.
Bad news. While you were recording that song it went gold, got played out and now people are burning you in effigy.
I shouldn't have taken that bathroom break
I have a secret. I'm a sucker for fake bands. Whenever The cast of "Saved by The Bell" shouldered their keytars and jam-synced some candy-ass tripe about friendship my smile could've broken my jaw. That said, these songs could be worse, no seriously, they'd be much more entertaining if they were. As is it's just warmed over Katy Perry. But what the hell do I know? I'm bitter & old. My daughter danced around like Kevin Bacon in a warehouse.
JEM
BEST MOVIE EVER!
TAKE That, "Frozen"!
But seriously get off the seats.
Actual review
©flickskinny inc 2015

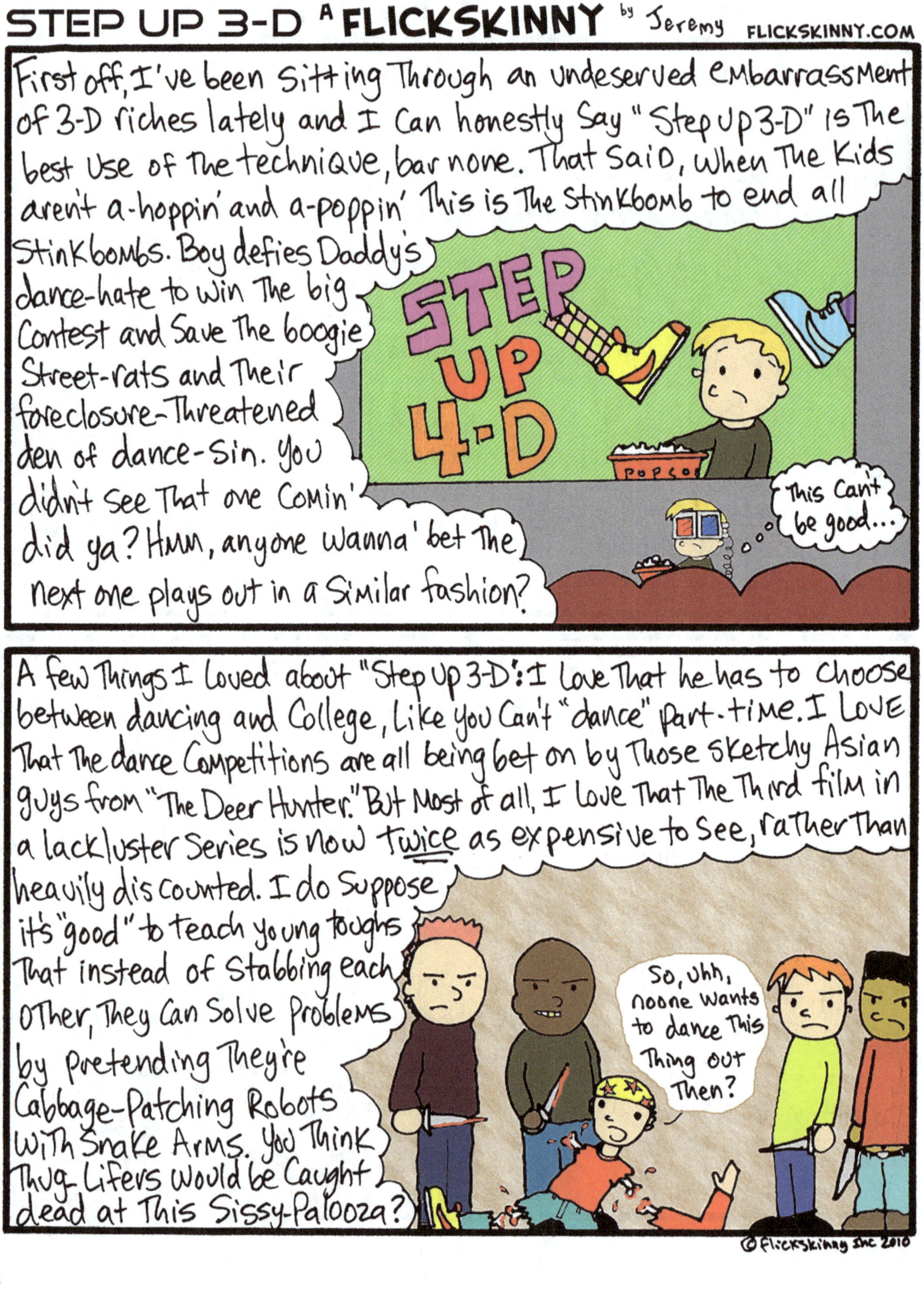
STEP UP 3-D A FLICKSKINNY by Jeremy
FLICKSKINNY.COM
First off, I've been sitting through an undeserved embarrassment of 3-D riches lately and I can honestly say "Step Up 3-D" is the best use of the technique, bar none. That said, when the kids aren't a-hoppin' and a-poppin' this is the stinkbomb to end all stinkbombs. Boy defies Daddy's dance-hate to win the big contest and save the boogie street-rats and their foreclosure-threatened den of dance-sin. You didn't see that one comin' did ya? Hmm, anyone wanna' bet the next one plays out in a similar fashion?
STEP UP 4-D
This can't be good...
A few things I loved about "Step Up 3-D": I love that he has to choose between dancing and college, like you can't "dance" part-time. I love that the dance competitions are all being bet on by those sketchy Asian guys from "The Deer Hunter." But most of all, I love that the third film in a lackluster series is now twice as expensive to see, rather than heavily discounted. I do suppose it's "good" to teach young toughs that instead of stabbing each other, they can solve problems by pretending they're Cabbage-Patching Robots with Snake Arms. You think Thug-Lifers would be caught dead at this Sissy-Palooza?
So, uhh, noone wants to dance this thing out then?
©Flickskinny Inc 2010

Sci-fi!

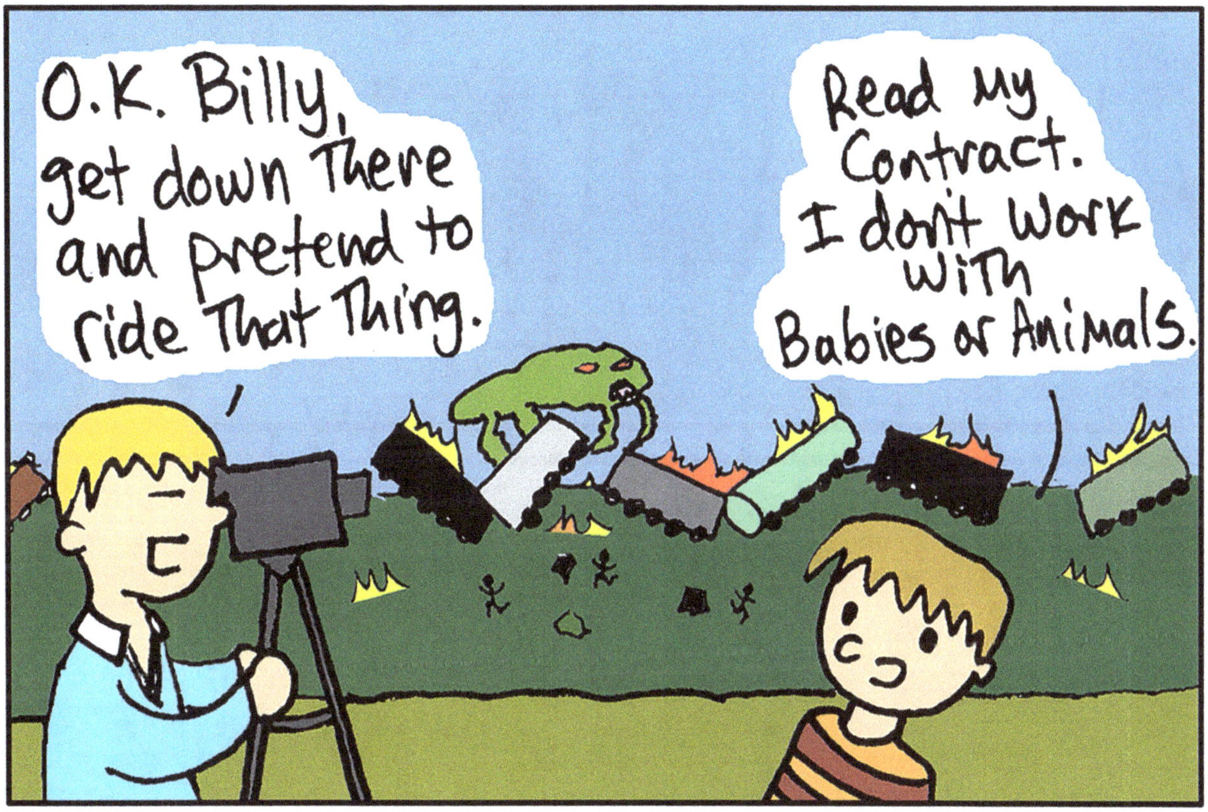
O.K. Billy, get down There and pretend to ride That Thing.
Read My Contract. I don't work with Babies or Animals.

The 5th Wave   The FLICKSKINNY by Jeremy

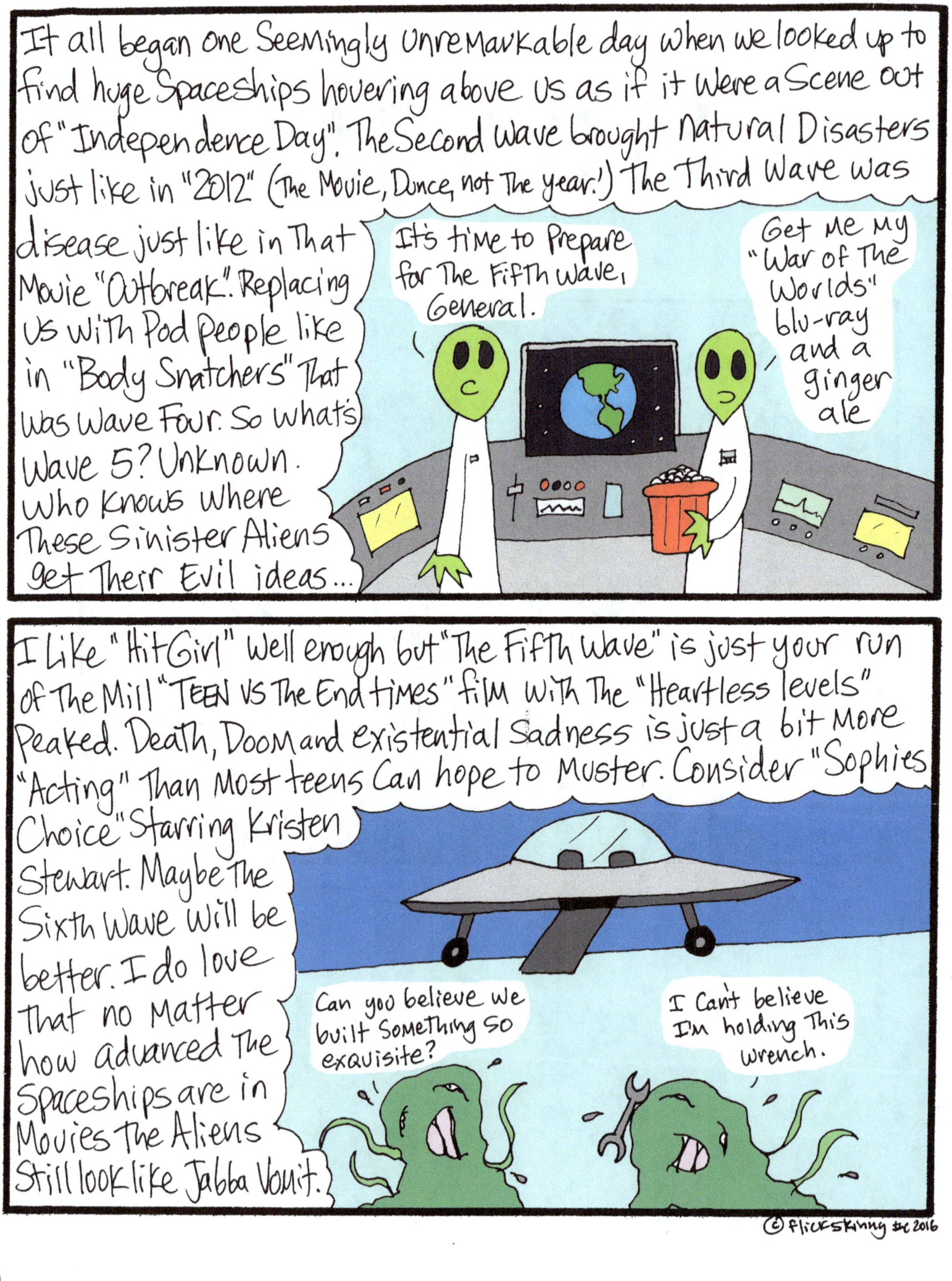

It all began one seemingly unremarkable day when we looked up to find huge spaceships hovering above us as if it were a scene out of "Independence Day". The second wave brought natural disasters just like in "2012" (The Movie, Dunce, not The year!) The Third Wave was disease just like in That Movie "Outbreak". Replacing us with Pod People like in "Body Snatchers" That was Wave Four. So what's Wave 5? Unknown. Who knows where These Sinister Aliens get Their Evil ideas...
It's time to Prepare for The Fifth wave, General.
Get Me My "War of The Worlds" blu-ray and a ginger ale
I Like "Hit Girl" well enough but "The Fifth Wave" is just your run of The Mill "TEEN VS The End times" film with The "Heartless levels" Peaked. Death, Doom and existential Sadness is just a bit More "Acting" Than Most teens Can hope to Muster. Consider "Sophies Choice" Starring Kristen Stewart. Maybe The Sixth Wave will be better. I do love That no Matter how advanced The Spaceships are in Movies The Aliens Still look like Jabba Vomit.
Can you believe we built Something so exquisite?
I Can't believe I'm holding This wrench.

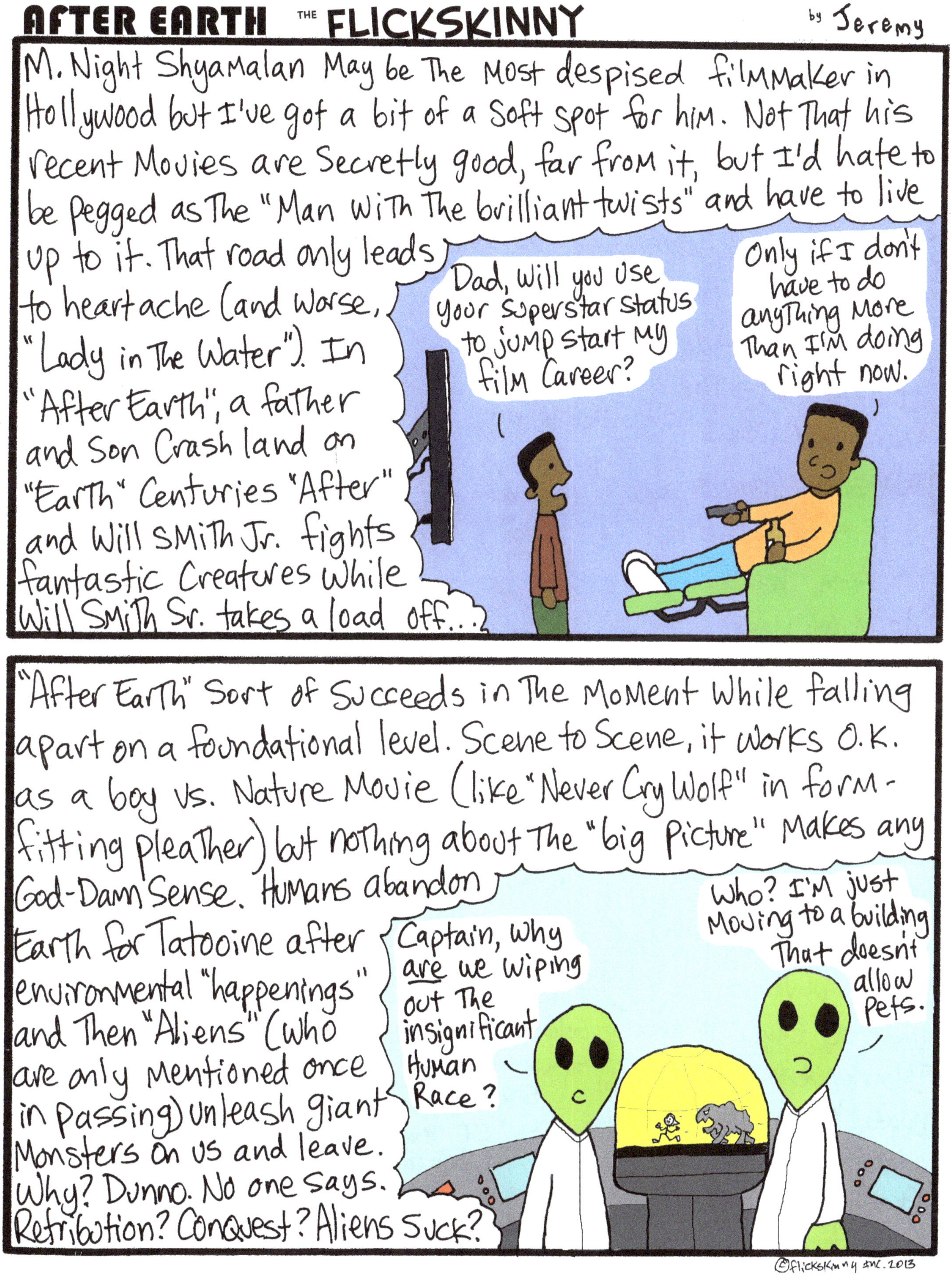
AFTER EARTH
THE FLICKSKINNY
by Jeremy
M. Night Shyamalan May be The Most despised filmmaker in Hollywood but I've got a bit of a Soft spot for him. Not That his recent Movies are Secretly good, far from it, but I'd hate to be pegged as The "Man With The brilliant twists" and have to live up to it. That road only leads to heartache (and worse, "Lady in The Water"). In "After Earth", a father and Son Crash land on "Earth" Centuries "After" and Will Smith Jr. fights fantastic Creatures while Will Smith Sr. takes a load off...
Dad, will you use your superstar status to jump start My film Career?
Only if I don't have to do anything More Than I'm doing right now.
"After Earth" Sort of Succeeds in The Moment While falling apart on a foundational level. Scene to Scene, it works O.K. as a boy vs. Nature Movie (like "Never Cry Wolf" in form-fitting pleather) but nothing about The "big Picture" Makes any God-Damn Sense. Humans abandon Earth for Tatooine after environmental "happenings" and Then "Aliens" (who are only mentioned once in passing) unleash giant Monsters on us and leave. Why? Dunno. No one says. Retribution? Conquest? Aliens Suck?
Captain, why are we wiping out The insignificant Human Race?
Who? I'm just Moving to a building That doesn't allow pets.
©flickskinny inc. 2013

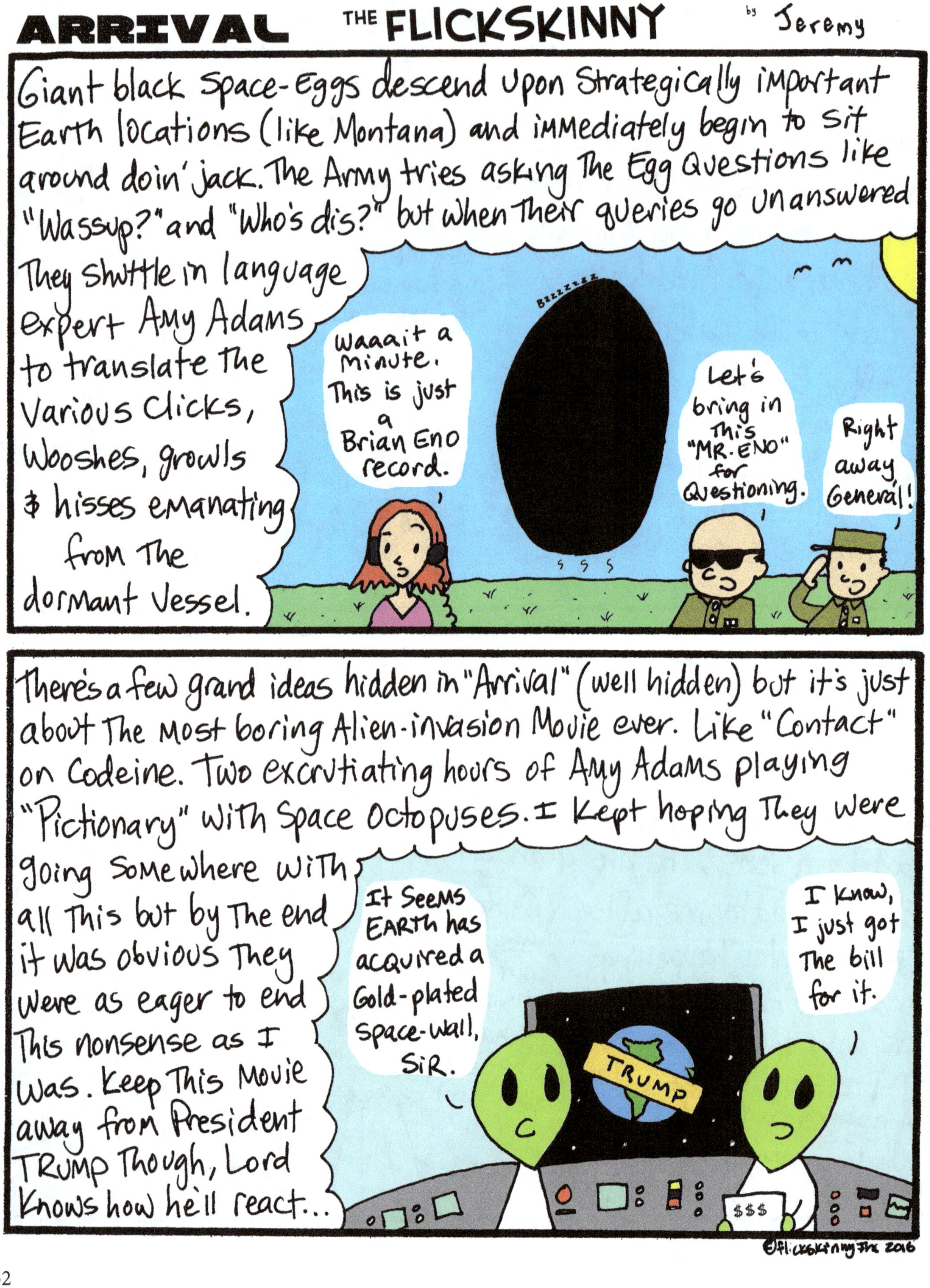
ARRIVAL
THE FLICKSKINNY
by Jeremy
Giant black Space-Eggs descend upon Strategically important Earth locations (like Montana) and immediately begin to sit around doin' jack. The Army tries asking The Egg Questions like "Wassup?" and "Who's dis?" but when Their queries go unanswered They shuttle in language expert Amy Adams to translate The Various Clicks, Wooshes, growls & hisses emanating from The dormant Vessel.
Bzzzzzzz
Waaait a minute. This is just a Brian Eno record.
Let's bring in This "MR. ENO" for Questioning.
Right away General!
There's a few grand ideas hidden in "Arrival" (well hidden) but it's just about The most boring Alien-invasion Movie ever. Like "Contact" on Codeine. Two excruciating hours of Amy Adams playing "Pictionary" with Space Octopuses. I kept hoping They were going somewhere with all This but by The end it was obvious They were as eager to end This nonsense as I was. Keep This Movie away from President TRUMP Though, Lord Knows how he'll react...
It Seems EARTH has acquired a Gold-plated Space-Wall, SiR.
I know, I just got The bill for it.
TRUMP
$$$
©Flickskinny Inc 2016

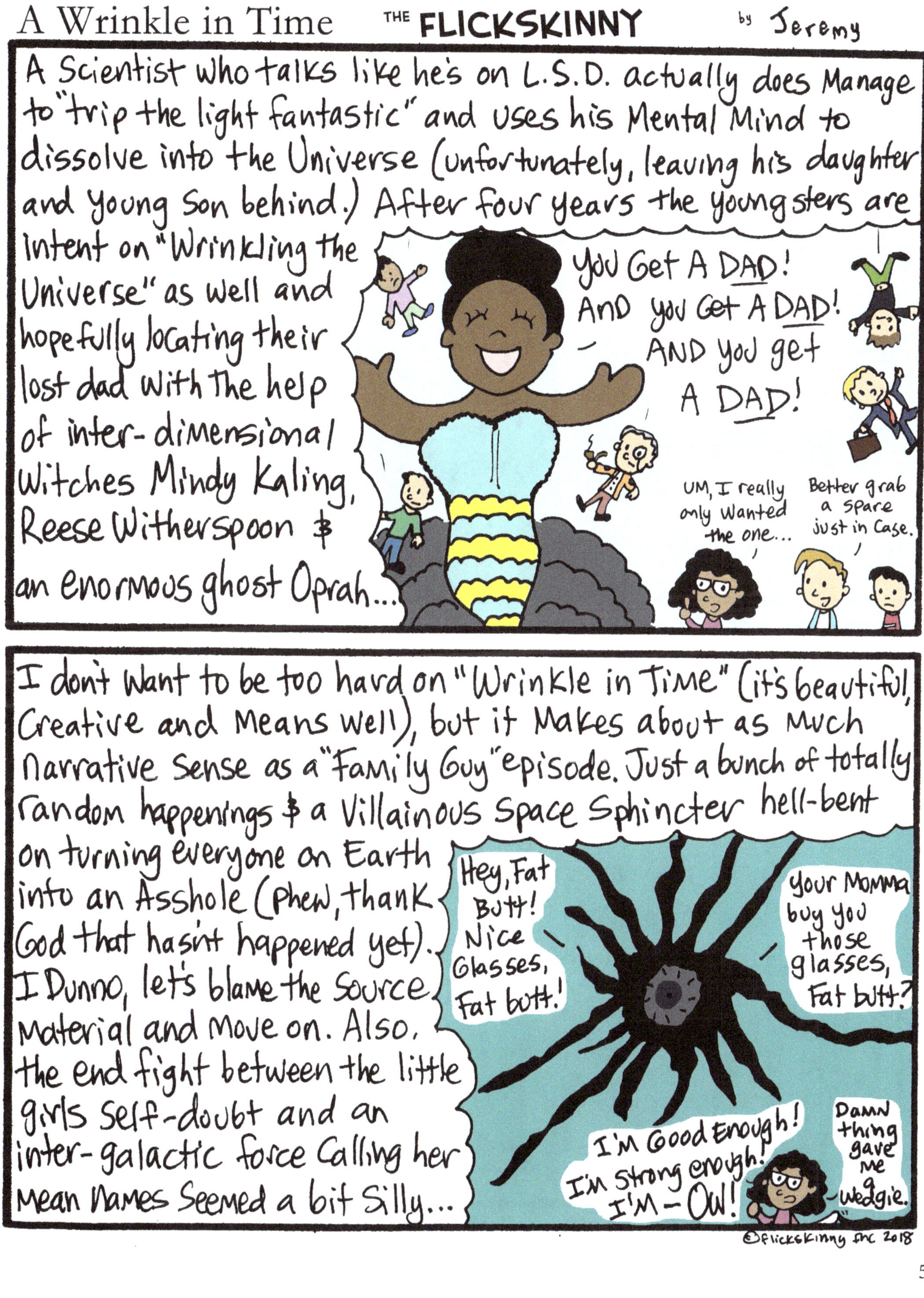
A Wrinkle in Time
THE FLICKSKINNY
by Jeremy
A Scientist who talks like he's on L.S.D. actually does Manage to "trip the light fantastic" and uses his Mental Mind to dissolve into the Universe (unfortunately, leaving his daughter and young Son behind.) After four years the youngsters are Intent on "Wrinkling the Universe" as well and hopefully locating their lost dad with the help of inter-dimensional Witches Mindy Kaling, Reese Witherspoon $ an enormous ghost Oprah...
You Get A DAD! AnD you Get A DAD! AND you get A DAD!
UM, I really only Wanted the one...
Better grab a spare just in Case.
I don't want to be too hard on "Wrinkle in Time" (it's beautiful, Creative and Means well), but it Makes about as Much narrative Sense as a "Family Guy" episode. Just a bunch of totally random happenings $ a Villainous Space Sphincter hell-bent on turning everyone on Earth into an Asshole (Phew, thank God that hasn't happened yet). I Dunno, let's blame the Source Material and Move on. Also, the end fight between the little girls Self-doubt and an inter-galactic force Calling her Mean Names Seemed a bit Silly...
Hey, Fat Butt! Nice Glasses, Fat butt!
Your Momma buy you those glasses, Fat butt?
I'M Good Enough! I'M Strong enough! I'M—OW!
Damn thing gave me a wedgie.
©flickskinny Inc 2018

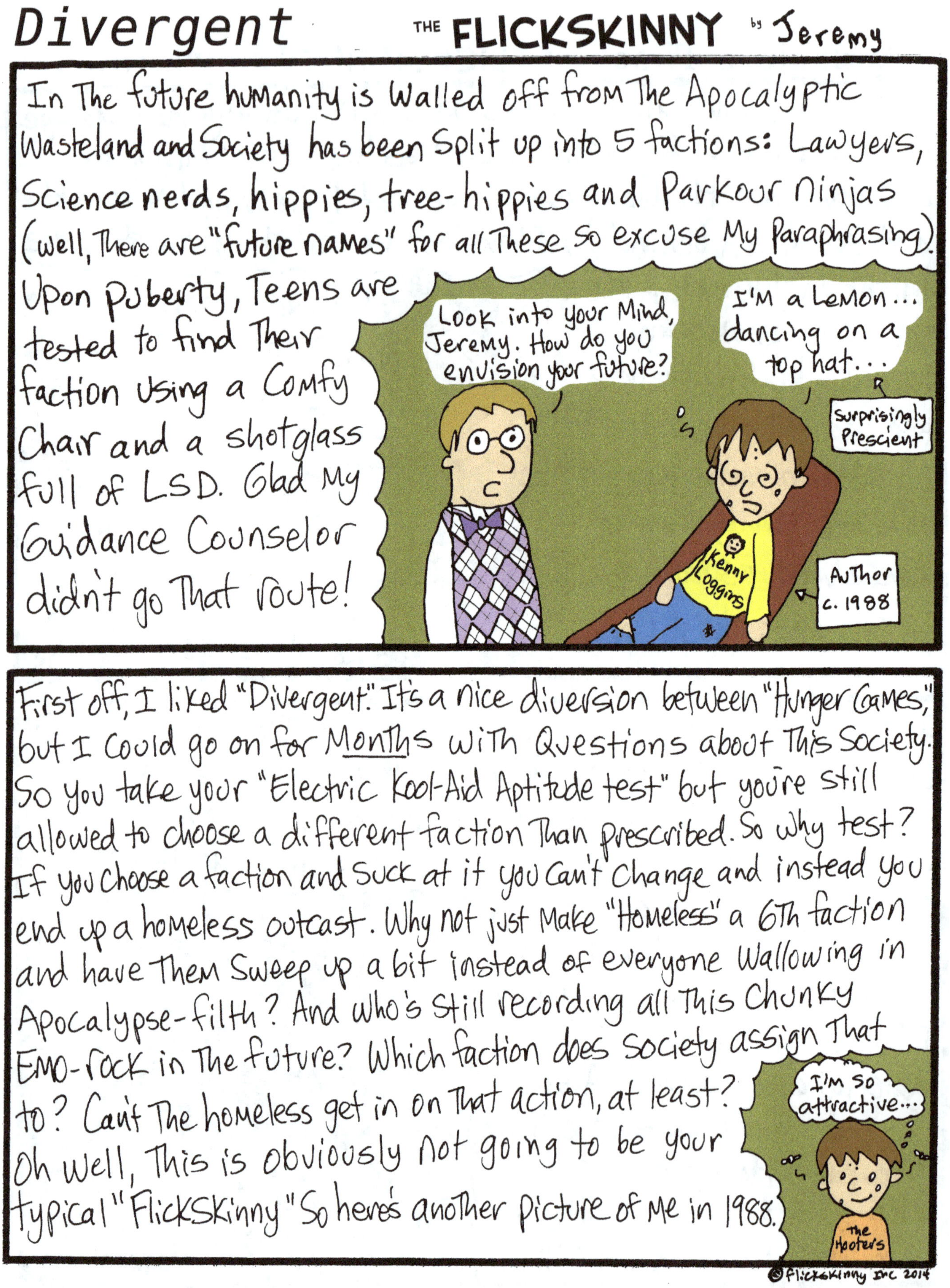
Divergent
THE FLICKSKINNY by Jeremy
In The future humanity is Walled off from The Apocalyptic Wasteland and Society has been Split up into 5 factions: Lawyers, Science nerds, hippies, tree-hippies and Parkour ninjas (well, There are "future names" for all These so excuse My Paraphrasing).
Upon puberty, Teens are tested to find Their faction using a Comfy Chair and a shotglass full of LSD. Glad My Guidance Counselor didn't go That route!
Look into your Mind, Jeremy. How do you envision your future?
I'M a LeMon... dancing on a top hat...
Surprisingly Prescient
Kenny Loggins
AuThor c. 1988
First off, I liked "Divergent." It's a nice diversion between "Hunger Games," but I Could go on for Months with Questions about This Society. So you take your "Electric Kool-Aid Aptitude test" but you're still allowed to choose a different faction Than prescribed. So why test? If you Choose a faction and Suck at it you Can't Change and instead you end up a homeless outcast. Why not just Make "Homeless" a 6Th faction and have Them Sweep up a bit instead of everyone Wallowing in Apocalypse-filth? And who's Still recording all This Chunky EMO-rock in The future? Which faction does Society assign That to? Can't The homeless get in on That action, at least? Oh well, This is obviously not going to be your typical "FlickSkinny" So here's another picture of Me in 1988.
I'M So attractive...
The Hooters
©FlickSkinny Inc 2014

Independence Day: Resurgence (2016) THE FLICKSKINNY by Jeremy

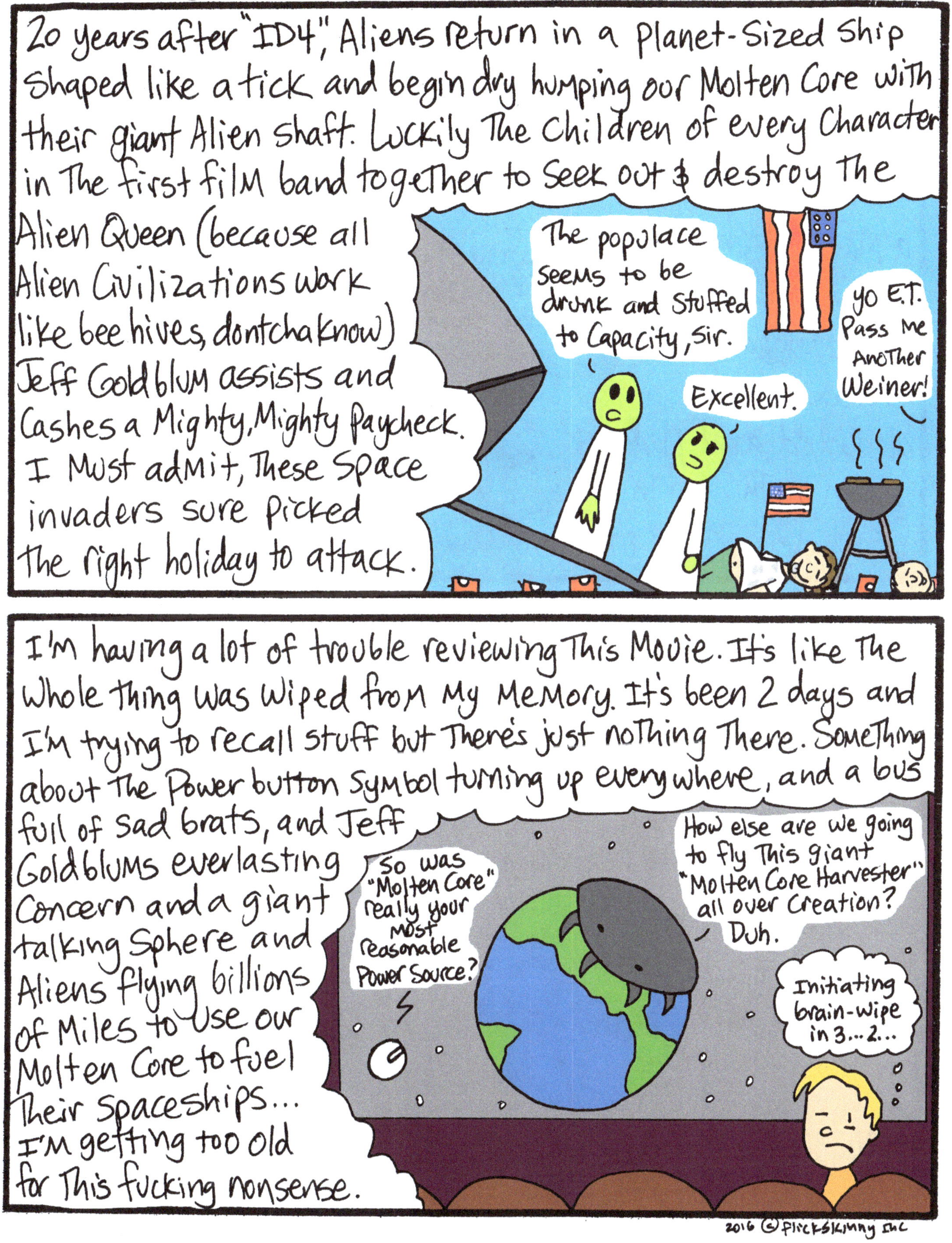
20 years after "ID4", Aliens return in a Planet-Sized Ship Shaped like a tick and begin dry humping our Molten Core with their giant Alien shaft. Luckily The Children of every Character in The first film band together to Seek out $ destroy The Alien Queen (because all Alien Civilizations work like bee hives, dontcha know) Jeff Goldblum assists and Cashes a Mighty, Mighty Paycheck. I Must admit, These Space invaders sure picked the right holiday to attack.
The populace seems to be drunk and stuffed to Capacity, Sir.
Excellent.
yo E.T. Pass Me Another Weiner!
I'm having a lot of trouble reviewing This Movie. It's like The Whole Thing was wiped from My Memory. It's been 2 days and I'm trying to recall stuff but There's just nothing There. Something about The Power button Symbol turning up everywhere, and a bus full of sad brats, and Jeff Goldblums everlasting Concern and a giant talking Sphere and Aliens flying billions of Miles to use our Molten Core to fuel Their Spaceships... I'M getting too old for This fucking nonsense.
So was "Molten Core" really your most reasonable Power Source?
How else are we going to fly This giant "Molten Core Harvester" all over Creation? Duh.
Initiating brain-wipe in 3... 2...
2016 © Flickskinny Inc

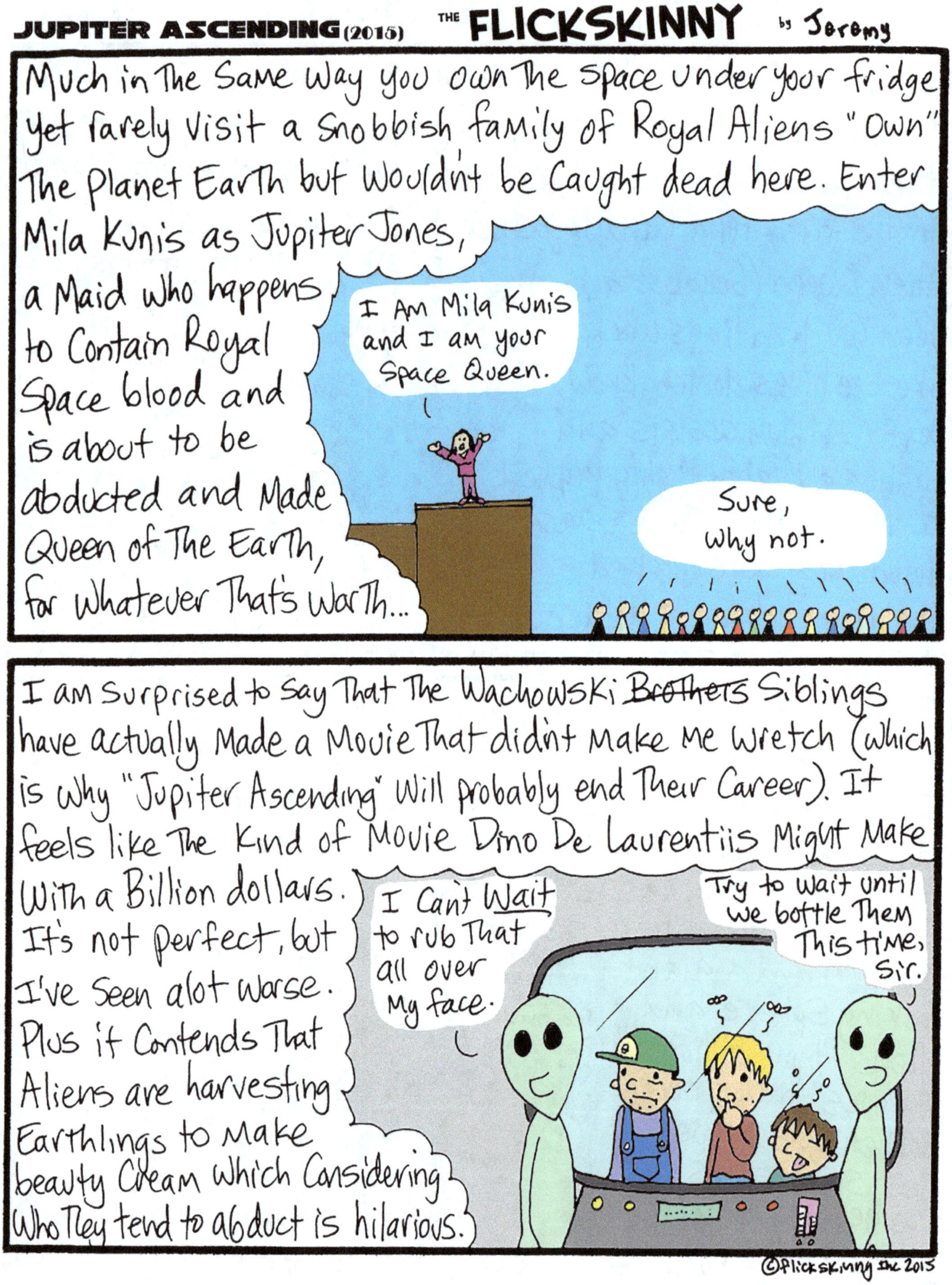
JUPITER ASCENDING (2015)
THE FLICKSKINNY by Jeremy
Much in The Same Way you own The space under your fridge yet rarely visit a snobbish family of Royal Aliens "own" The planet Earth but wouldn't be caught dead here. Enter Mila Kunis as Jupiter Jones, a Maid who happens to Contain Royal Space blood and is about to be abducted and Made Queen of The Earth, for whatever That's worth...
I Am Mila Kunis and I am your Space Queen.
Sure, why not.
I am Surprised to Say That The Wachowski ~~Brothers~~ Siblings have actually Made a Movie That didn't Make Me wretch (which is why "Jupiter Ascending" Will probably end Their Career). It feels like The Kind of Movie Dino De Laurentiis Might Make With a Billion dollars. It's not perfect, but I've Seen alot worse. Plus it Contends That Aliens are harvesting Earthlings to Make beauty Cream which Considering Who They tend to abduct is hilarious.
I Can't Wait to rub That all over My face.
Try to wait until we bottle Them This time, Sir.
©Flickskinny Inc 2015

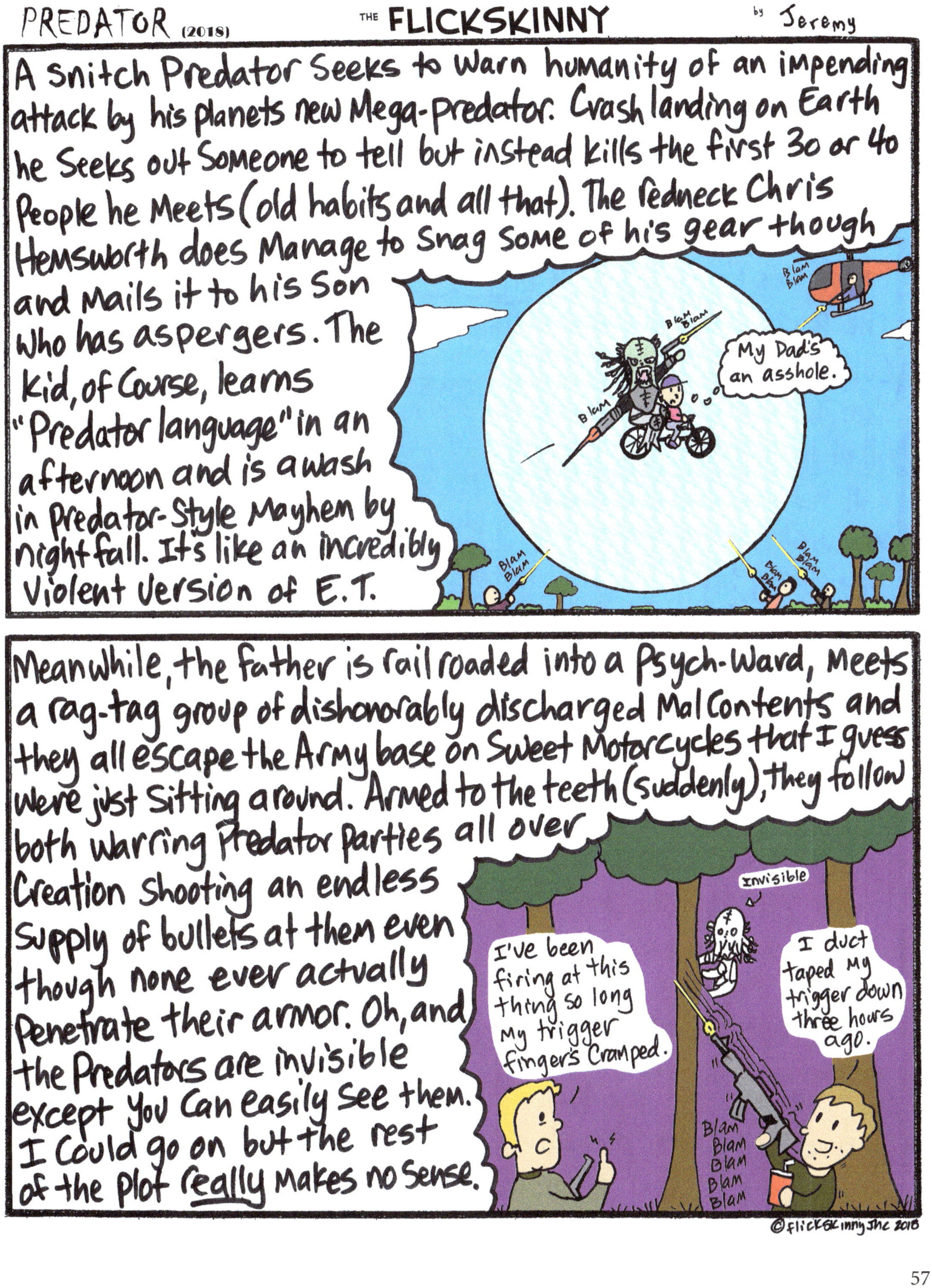
PREDATOR (2018)
THE FLICKSKINNY
by Jeremy
A snitch Predator Seeks to warn humanity of an impending attack by his planets new Mega-predator. Crash landing on Earth he Seeks out Someone to tell but instead kills the first 30 or 40 People he Meets (old habits and all that). The redneck Chris Hemsworth does Manage to Snag some of his gear though and Mails it to his Son who has aspergers. The kid, of Course, learns "Predator language" in an afternoon and is awash in Predator-Style Mayhem by nightfall. It's like an incredibly Violent Version of E.T.
Blam Blam
Blam Blam
My Dad's an asshole.
Blam
Blam Blam
Blam Blam
Blam Blam
Meanwhile, the father is railroaded into a Psych-Ward, Meets a rag-tag group of dishonorably discharged MalContents and they all escape the Army base on Sweet Motorcycles that I guess were just Sitting around. Armed to the teeth (suddenly), they follow both warring Predator parties all over Creation shooting an endless Supply of bullets at them even though none ever actually Penetrate their armor. Oh, and the Predators are invisible except you Can easily see them. I Could go on but the rest of the plot really makes no sense.
Invisible
I've been firing at this thing so long my trigger finger's Cramped.
I duct taped my trigger down three hours ago.
Blam Blam Blam Blam Blam
©FlickSkinny Inc 2018

READY PLAYER ONE
THE FLICKSKINNY by Jeremy

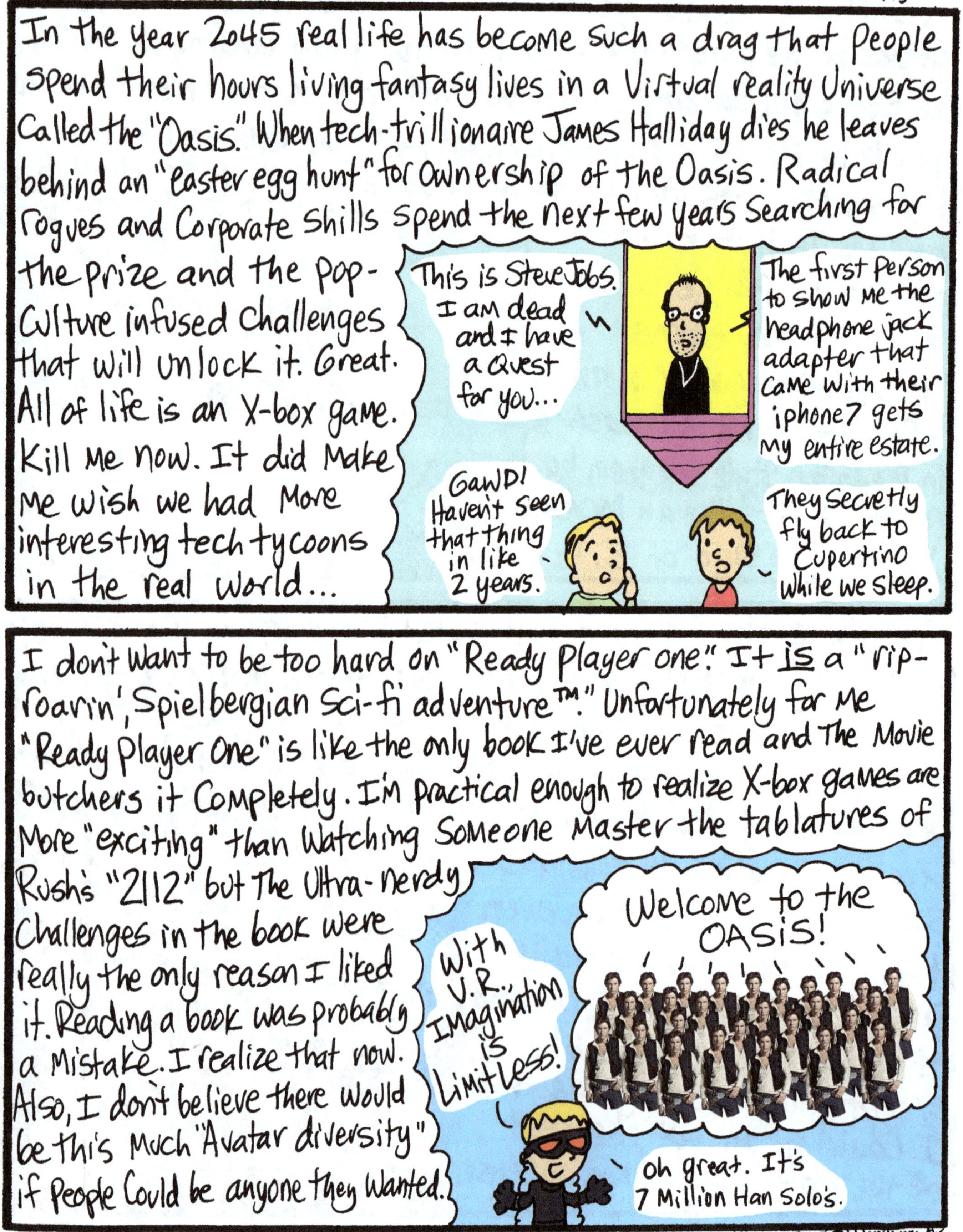
In the year 2045 real life has become such a drag that people spend their hours living fantasy lives in a Virtual reality Universe Called the "Oasis." When tech-trillionaire James Halliday dies he leaves behind an "easter egg hunt" for ownership of the Oasis. Radical rogues and Corporate Shills spend the next few years searching for the prize and the pop-culture infused challenges that will unlock it. Great. All of life is an X-box game. Kill me now. It did make me wish we had more interesting tech tycoons in the real world...
This is Steve Jobs. I am dead and I have a Quest for you...
The first person to show me the headphone jack adapter that came with their iphone7 gets my entire estate.
GAWD! Haven't seen that thing in like 2 years.
They secretly fly back to Cupertino while we sleep.
I don't want to be too hard on "Ready Player one." It is a "rip-roarin', Spielbergian Sci-fi adventure™." Unfortunately for me "Ready Player One" is like the only book I've ever read and The Movie butchers it Completely. I'm practical enough to realize X-box games are more "exciting" than watching someone master the tablatures of Rush's "2112" but the Ultra-nerdy challenges in the book were really the only reason I liked it. Reading a book was probably a mistake. I realize that now. Also, I don't believe there would be this much "Avatar diversity" if people could be anyone they wanted.
With V.R., Imagination is Limitless!
Welcome to the OASIS!
oh great. It's 7 Million Han Solo's.

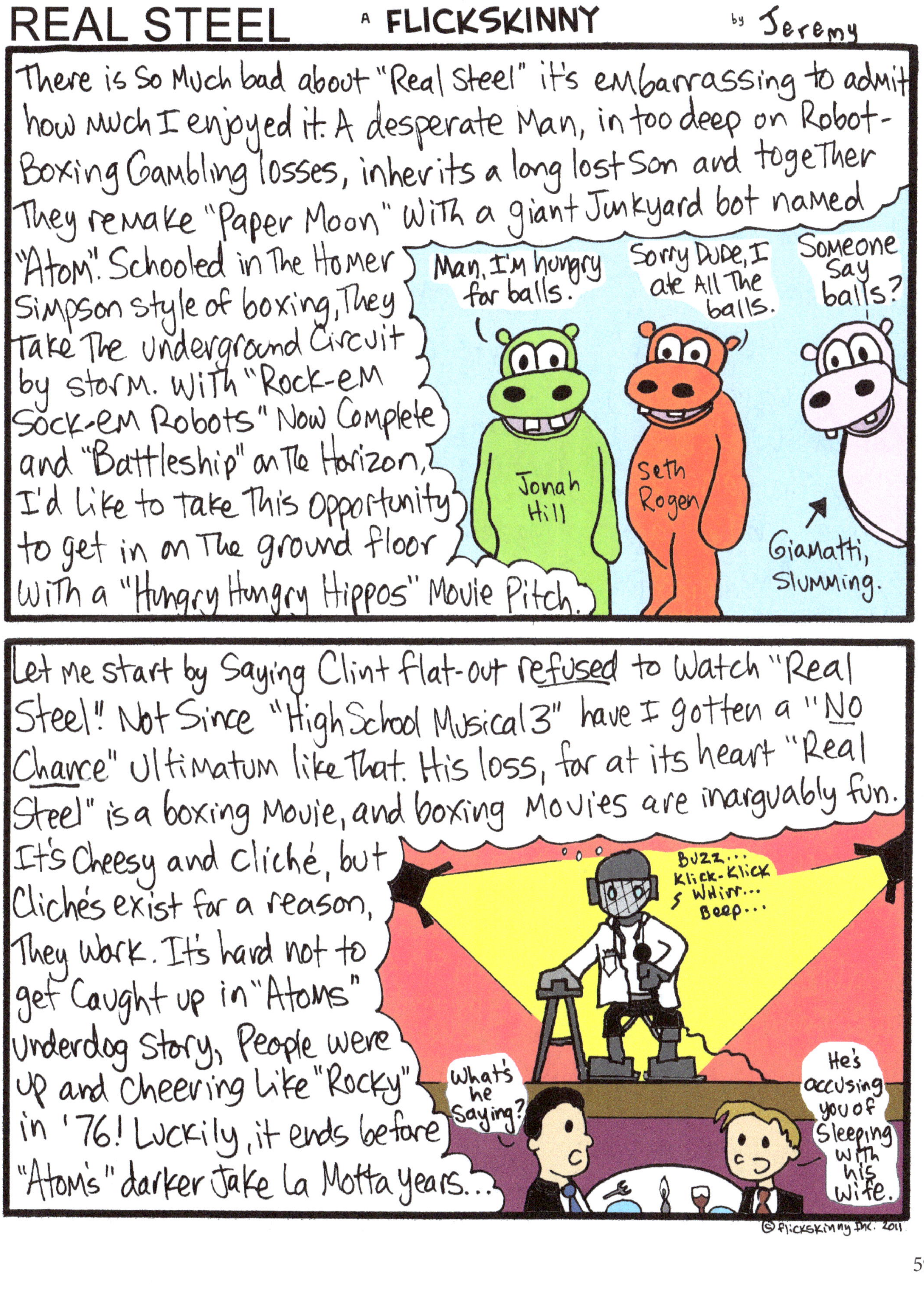
REAL STEEL
a FLICKSKINNY
by Jeremy
There is So Much bad about "Real Steel" it's embarrassing to admit how much I enjoyed it. A desperate Man, in too deep on Robot-Boxing Gambling losses, inherits a long lost Son and together They remake "Paper Moon" With a giant Junkyard bot named "Atom". Schooled in The Homer Simpson style of boxing, They Take The underground Circuit by storm. With "Rock-em Sock-em Robots" Now Complete and "Battleship" on The Horizon, I'd like to take This opportunity to get in on The ground floor With a "Hungry Hungry Hippos" Movie Pitch.
Man, I'm hungry for balls.
Sorry Dude, I ate All The balls.
Someone Say balls?
Jonah Hill
Seth Rogen
Giamatti, Slumming.
Let me start by Saying Clint flat-out refused to Watch "Real Steel"! Not Since "High School Musical 3" have I gotten a "No Chance" Ultimatum like That. His loss, for at its heart "Real Steel" is a boxing Movie, and boxing Movies are inarguably fun.
It's Cheesy and cliché, but Clichés exist for a reason, They Work. It's hard not to get Caught up in "Atoms" underdog Story, People were up and Cheering like "Rocky" in '76! Luckily, it ends before "Atom's" darker Jake La Motta years...
Buzz... Klick-Klick Whirr... Beep...
What's he saying?
He's accusing you of Sleeping with his Wife.
© Flickskinny Inc. 2011

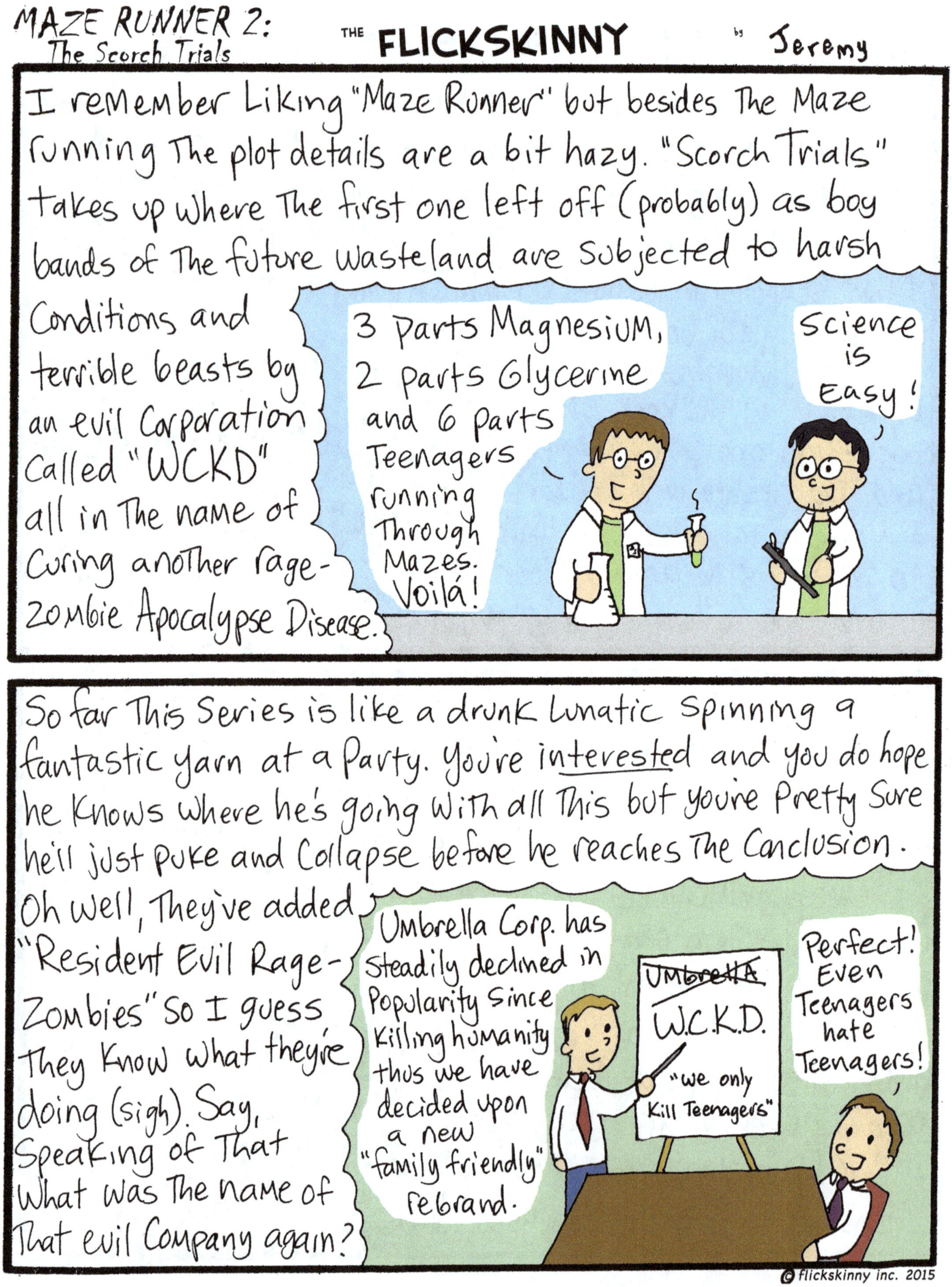

MAZE RUNNER 2: The Scorch Trials
THE FLICKSKINNY by Jeremy
I remember Liking "Maze Runner" but besides The Maze running The plot details are a bit hazy. "Scorch Trials" takes up where The first one left off (probably) as boy bands of The future wasteland are Subjected to harsh Conditions and terrible beasts by an evil Corporation Called "WCKD" all in The name of Curing another rage-zombie Apocalypse Disease.
3 parts Magnesium, 2 parts Glycerine and 6 parts Teenagers running Through Mazes. Voilá!
Science is Easy!
So far This Series is like a drunk Lunatic Spinning a fantastic yarn at a Party. You're interested and you do hope he Knows where he's going With all This but you're Pretty Sure he'll just puke and Collapse before he reaches The Conclusion.
Oh well, They've added "Resident Evil Rage-Zombies" So I guess They Know what they're doing (sigh). Say, Speaking of That What was The name of That evil Company again?
Umbrella Corp. has Steadily declined in Popularity Since Killing humanity thus we have decided upon a new "family friendly" rebrand.
UMbrellA
W.C.K.D.
"we only Kill Teenagers"
Perfect! Even Teenagers hate Teenagers!
© flickskinny inc. 2015

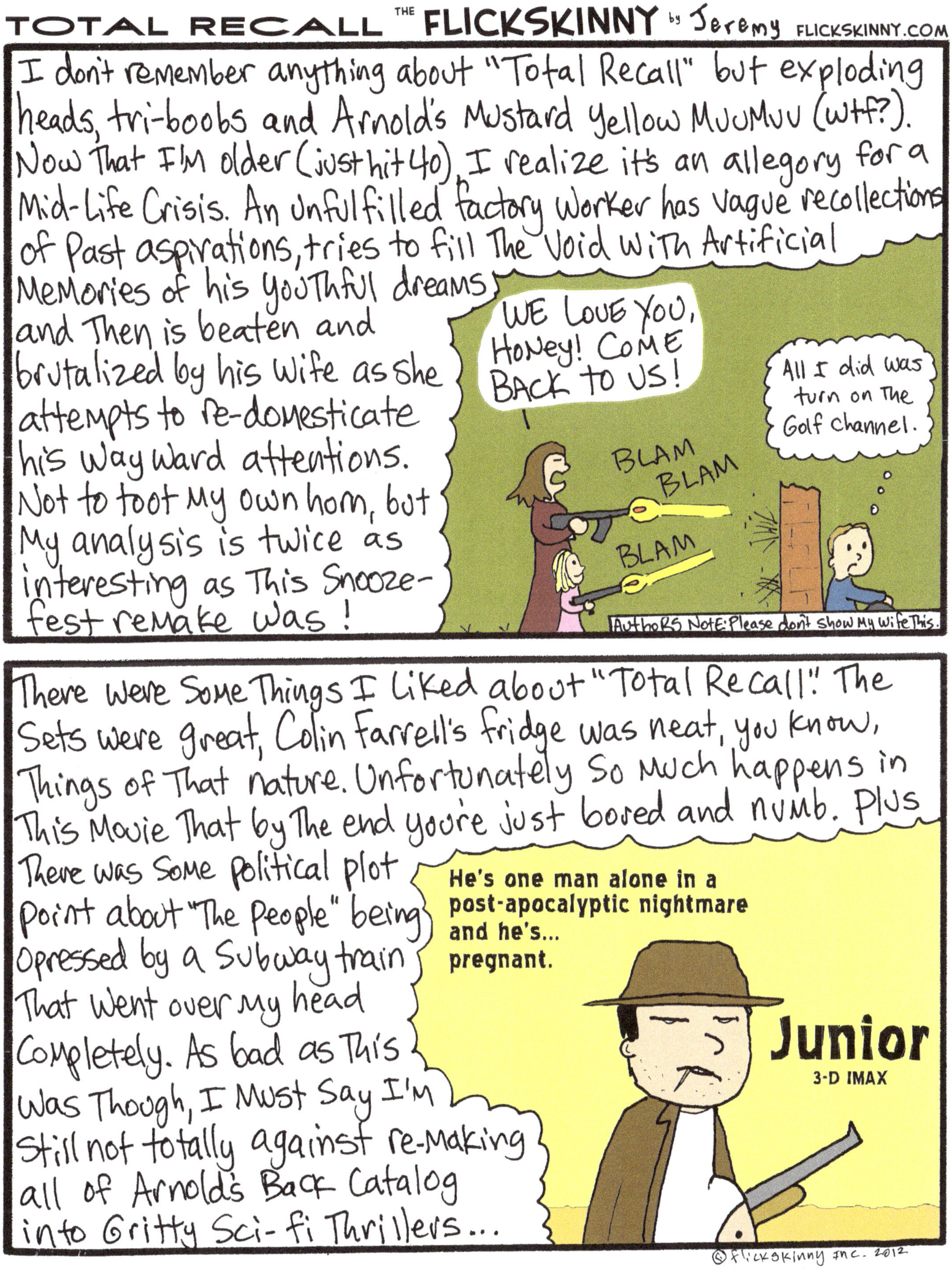
TOTAL RECALL
THE FLICKSKINNY by Jeremy
FLICKSKINNY.COM
I don't remember anything about "Total Recall" but exploding heads, tri-boobs and Arnold's Mustard Yellow MuuMuu (wtf?). Now That I'M older (just hit 40), I realize it's an allegory for a Mid-Life Crisis. An unfulfilled factory worker has vague recollections of Past aspirations, tries to fill The Void With Artificial Memories of his youThful dreams and Then is beaten and brutalized by his Wife as she attempts to re-domesticate his wayward attentions. Not to toot My own horn, but My analysis is twice as interesting as This Snooze-fest remake was!
WE LOVE YOU, HONEY! COME BACK TO US!
All I did was turn on The Golf channel.
BLAM
BLAM
BLAM
AuthoRS NotE: Please don't show My wife This.
There were Some Things I Liked about "Total Recall." The Sets were great, Colin Farrell's fridge was neat, you know, Things of That nature. Unfortunately So Much happens in This Movie That by The end you're just bored and numb. Plus There was Some political plot point about "The People" being opressed by a Subway train That went over My head Completely. As bad as This was Though, I Must Say I'M Still not totally against re-Making all of Arnold's Back Catalog into Gritty Sci-fi Thrillers...
He's one man alone in a post-apocalyptic nightmare and he's... pregnant.
Junior
3-D IMAX
©flickskinny Inc. 2012

www.ingramcontent.com/pod-product-compliance
Lightning Source LLC
Chambersburg PA
CBHW060427010526
44118CB00017B/2394